The Open Letter of Apology to the World

and some other sad stuff

God help us.
We're in such big trouble.

from Doug Perry
Fellowship Of The Martyrs

**FELLOWSHIP
OF THE
MARTYRS**

The Bride gets her jewelry, but it's going to hurt to get it on,
and once you're used to it, you're never going to want to
rip it back off again. Heaven is free. HOLINESS is hard!
If not us, who? If not here, where? If not now, when?

DEDICATION

This book is dedicated to Jesus Christ.
In fact, everything I've written, recorded, sung,
spoken or ever done is dedicated to Jesus Christ.
Not that it was all perfect, but that's not His fault.
If you don't like it, blame me, not Him.

I want to take special note of the people who were so
instrumental in helping grow me. Some were used to
encourage me, some were used to teach me patience, some
were used by God to motivate me to find the demon on them
that I might never have seen if they weren't on my last nerve.
Some taught me to endure persecution, even from the closest
friend. Some showed me holiness. Praise God! They were all
a blessing in one way or another and I really do love them all.
(You know which one you were.)

Bob, Nancy, David, Marilyn, Kim, Constance, Stephanie, Ric, Brad,
Keith, Steve, Minnie, Jeannie and Stevie, Andrew, Rachael, Elijah,
Bob, Clare, Gary, Kristi, James, Cindy, Helen, Sherri, Jen, Dennis,
Merri, Joseph, Gary, Cary, Emily, Lili, David, Yolanda, Suzanne,
Tabitha, Josh, Austin, Chris, Candi, Nataliya, Helen, Ron, Rusty,
Josh, Barry, Barron, Glynda, Steve, Bianca, June, Andrew, John,
Lisa, Diane, Larry, Dewey, Jason, Sarah, Dave, Doug, Michael,
Nichole, Dorothy, Tyler, Ky, Kathy, Lizzie, Patrick, Sharon, Stevean,
Randy, Bob, Casey, Amy, Cathy, Chuckie, Roger, Nils, Ryan, Shelly,
Kurt, Sharon, John, Mikey, Becky, James, Jennie, Angela, Gus, Zach,
Jason, Jacob, Greg, Tres, Daniel, J.R., Tatianna, Patti and Carolyn
and HUNDREDS that I pray will not feel left out but I don't have room
to mention.

And a couple million intercessors all over the world pouring
their hearts out and crying rivers on our behalf without whom
I'm not sure how we could have made it this far.
I'm humbled. Please don't stop praying.

I love you all and I'm not going to stop no matter what.

CONTENTS

ACKNOWLEDGMENTS

I want to thank Jesus Christ. Without Him I'm nothing. This is all about Him and not about me. Everything good that I have learned came from Him. Everything false that I have learned came from Man – me included. God used some people to speak His Truth to me and I'm grateful to all of them as well for their obedience. God also used some people to speak lies to me so that I would learn how to tell the difference, and I'm grateful for them as well. I'm also grateful to the folks that were oppressed by demons so that we could learn and practice on them.

If you don't know Jesus, if you're not talking to Him every day and communing with Him and letting Him direct all your paths, then you're missing out on the greatest adventure in history! And you're totally defenseless against the spiritual wickedness in high places that is in charge of this world. And there is no peace and joy and victory without being all the way full of Jesus. We're getting to the end of The Book. Bad stuff is coming and you're going to need all the peace that passes understanding that you can get! You might want to hurry.

If you don't have Him, then you need Him. If you need Him and we can help, please get in touch with us and we'll introduce you to Him. He doesn't just want Sundays and Wednesday nights – if you open your heart to Him, do it in as big a way as possible. Give Him ALL right up front and see what He does with you.

Push ALL your chips out onto the table and bet it ALL on God – every single time. He'll back you up.

i

OPEN LETTER OF
APOLOGY TO THE WORLD

Please bear with me, this is long overdue and there's lots of ground to cover. I want to make sure that I get it all out. Not just for me, but because I think you need to hear it. Maybe there are other Christians out there as well that need to make apologies and will find courage here. I appreciate your time, I know it's valuable.

Dear Members of the World,

I'm just a guy, nobody really. Son of a preacher and missionary. Years and years of Vacation Bible Schools, summer camps, youth ski trips, puppet shows, revivals, choir trips - you name it. Even went to a Christian college and got a degree in religion. I ended up in the business world, but I spent two decades tithing, sitting on committees, teaching Sunday School, going to seminars and conferences, etc. I even met my wife in the single's class at church. I'm not a bad guy, I've been mostly

1

behaving myself and everybody seems to like me. I do some good stuff here and there.

But lately I've been trying to understand Jesus more and stuff I never noticed before has really started to bug me. I've been taking a look around and I'm having a hard time making sense of what it is we've built here. So, it just seemed like, whether anybody else says it or not, I need to take responsibility for the part I played and say what I have to say.

Here we go ...

I know you think that Christians are a big bunch of hypocrites. We say we're more "religious" and we're going to heaven and you're not, and then we drive our big shiny cars with little fishies on the trunk and cut you off in traffic as we race by the homeless guy on the corner. We average just 2% of our money to church and charity, despite that we say the Bible is the word of God and **it** says we're supposed to give **everything**. On average, we buy just as many big screen TVs and bass boats and fur coats and makeup and baseball cards and online porn as anybody else. Maybe more. You've seen leader after leader end up in jail or court or a sex scandal of one sort or another.

Well ... you're right. We're guilty of all of it. We've done it all. And, I'm really sorry.

You see our cheesy TV shows and slick guys begging for money and you get that there's something seriously sneaky and wrong here. A high-pressure call for money so they can stay on the air? Were we supposed to use Jesus as just another form of entertainment? Who do we think we're kidding? Where's Jesus in all this? Aren't we supposed to rely on him? Isn't He going to meet our needs if we're inside His will? What happened to sacrifice and suffering and helping the poor? I'm just sick about this. I mean, the church leaders, they're not all bad guys, there are lots and lots of really hard-working well-meaning folks who love and care and are meeting real needs in the community. Some of them understand and love Jesus - but I'm just real sure those pastors don't drive Bentley's, have multi-million dollar homes and their own Lear jets! I mean, what "god" are we worshiping? Money? Ego? Power?

You see our massive shiny new buildings all over the place. Heck, maybe we even kicked you out of your house so we could expand our parking lots. You can't figure out why we need four different Christian churches on four corners of the same intersection. We've got playgrounds and bowling alleys and basketball leagues. We've got Starbucks coffee in the sanctuary. We've got orchestras and giant chandeliers and fountains out front. We've got bookstores full of "jesus junk" with every imaginable style and flavor of religious knick-knack. But where's Jesus? Is this what HE wanted?

Oh, sure, there are good folks all over and not every church is such a mess, but Christians are the ones that say we're supposed to be "One Body." So even the good ones are guilty of not putting a stop to it sooner. We were supposed to keep each other in line and not tolerate factions and dissensions and greed and idolatry and all this other bad stuff. Man, we really blew it! We've got 33,000 denominations and most of them won't talk to the other ones. We lose over $5 million a day to fraud from "trusted" people inside the church! We spend 95% of all our money on our own comforts and programs and happy family fun

3

ne shows and we let 250 MILLION Christians in other countries live on the very edge of starvation. Not to mention the billion or so that have never even once heard of Jesus - or the homeless guy downtown we almost ran over when we cut you off.

We're as guilty as we can be. All of us. Nobody is exempt. We should have put a stop to it a lot sooner. But I can't apologize on behalf of anyone else. This is about me.

I know that you might have gone to church as a kid and stopped going as soon as you could. I know that you might even have been abused by somebody in the church! Maybe we got you all fired up and then just let you drift off like we didn't really care. Maybe you just don't fit our "profile." You might have piercings and purple hair or tattoos or been in jail -- and somewhere inside you just know that even if you wanted to go to church one Sunday, it would not go well. I'm sorry for that. Jesus loves you. He always hung out with the most unexpected people. He had the biggest heart for the folks everybody else tried to ignore. What have we done? We've told you to put on a sweater and some loafers or you can't go to heaven. I just want to throw up.

Look, I know you're mad. And you have a right to be. We've done you wrong for a LONG time now. There's some things about Jesus that people need to hear, but we've buried a beautiful masterpiece under hundreds of layers of soft pink latex paint. If you have a Bible handy, look up Matthew 23. (If you don't, you can look it up here - BibleGateway.com .)

Find it? Read it carefully, the Pharisees were the "religious" people of the day, the leaders of the faith. In this chapter Jesus SEVEN times says how pitiful and wretched and cursed they are for what they're doing to the people they're supposed to be leading. He even calls them "white washed tombs of dead mens bones" and a "brood of vipers"! I don't have time here, but read it and see if we're not doing EVERY single one of those things. Jesus can't possibly be happy about what we've done to you.

Sure, we like to kid ourselves and pretend everything is OK - but it's not. We're hated. Now, please understand, Jesus was hated, too. But that was because he said hard things and sometimes people don't like hearing the Truth. And he promised we would be hated if we were like him. But that's not why we're hated at the moment. We're hated right now because we're a giant pack of lying hypocrites that say one thing and do something else altogether. If we were hated because we were like Jesus, that would be one thing, but that's not it at all. You see right through our happy music and fluffy services and you can tell there's something desperately wrong here. We're no different than anybody else - except that we say we're better than you.

It was never supposed to be like this. Jesus asked us to care for the widows and orphans, to feed the hungry, care for the sick, visit those in prison, reach the lost. He wanted us to love our enemies and pray for them. He cared about human justice and suffering, the lost and lonely. But I don't think He would have marched on a picket line - He had His mind on much bigger problems. He wanted us to focus on the eternal things, not the everyday. He never once said to go into all the world and build big buildings and divide up into factions and buy Bentleys. Just the opposite! I get that you're mad at us and I think you have a right to be, but please understand, you're mad at what we've made under our own power, you're mad at "Churchianity." That's different than Christ and what he wanted. Don't be mad at Jesus! This mess wasn't His idea!

5

Look, I'm really sorry. I accept responsibility for my part in having hurt you. But I'm committing to you all, dear Members of the World, that I'm not going to do it any more. Not a single penny more. I'm not going to put my faith in "Churchianity" or any leader or program or TV show -- but in Christ Jesus and His salvation. That's when I was set free and began to see that God wants and expects more of us than this. And I'm not helping anybody that's not fully committed to the same thing.

It took centuries to build this monster, so it's not like it's going to just turn around overnight. But the times are changing and we're way overdue for something new. Big bad things are happening - like the tsunami in Asia - and I think more are coming. I don't want any more time to go by without having said this. I'm sorry for all the time and money I've wasted. But Jesus saves. Really. The church itself isn't even the point. Jesus is the real deal. He lived and He died for my sins and He rose again. He is who He said He was and He cares about me - and you. He's our only hope. We need places you can go that will only teach Jesus and will not be swayed or tempted or distracted by anything else. God willing, that's coming.

Please don't think all Christians are just posers. Some of them really mean it when they say they belong to Christ. The problem is mostly in the West where we're all comfy and complacent and seem to like it that way. The Christians in China and other places are deadly serious. There's no room for anything but Jesus when you're on the run from the government. They are dying every day for their faith and doing crazy hard things because they're absolutely committed to Christ. These are martyrs. People willing to crucify little pieces of themselves every day to be more like

Christ. People willing to set aside everything they want, to do what Christ wants. People willing to rot in prison or take a beating or die if that's what it's going to take. People that act in pure love and never back down. I'm not worthy to tie their shoes. And there are some like that here, too, and I hope we can get a lot more people to start living that way. It's way overdue.

If you're talking to someone and they tell you they're a Christian, ask them if they're the kind of Christian that really means it all the time or the kind that just means it on Sunday. The Bible says we'll know them by their "fruits" - by the faith and purity and love in their deeds and words. When you find one that proves Christ is in them by how much they love you, ask them to tell you all about Jesus. If you know one of those fearless martyrs that speaks nothing but pure, clean, hard Truth - ask lots of questions. Truth is a lot more rare than you would think. But don't settle for soft, fluffy and comfortable anymore - that's not in the Bible.

As for me and my house, we're really sorry. From now on, we're going to serve the Lord, not "Churchianity." We're going to try to call together as many of those martyrs as we can and start doing what Christ wanted. If I run into you someday, please give me a chance to shake your hand and apologize in person. I'm going to try harder from now on, I promise. I think there are lots of others feeling the same way, so don't be surprised if you start hearing stuff like this more often.

Thanks for your time. I hope it helps.

Doug Perry
fotm@fellowshipofthemartyrs.com

WHY THE APOLOGY TO THE WORLD?

Well, first off, I wrote it because I really mean it. I am seriously sorry for what I did to contribute to this mess and I'm determined to do whatever I can to fix it. So ... the more help I can get, the faster we can turn this thing around. So if it happens that lots of other folks get a little courage and see that this needs saying, maybe they'll say it, too. I've repented to God already for it and He's forgiven me, but that doesn't mean I don't have to humbly ask forgiveness from everybody else.

I believe this is the "elephant in the room" that everybody knows is there but doesn't want to acknowledge. The World despises Christians - and Christians know that they're despised. It's just that the Christians aren't admitting the real problem. A lot of them get that there IS a problem, but they don't know how to say it loud enough to get some momentum.

Truth is always the right answer. Truth is getting scarce lately. When folks hear it, it's so unusual that they perk up and see if it was an accident or a scam or a publicity stunt -- but inside they hope they get more chances to hear it. People are desperate for someone that will not make excuses and will not back down. We've had about all the self-serving "spin" we can take.

I think this is the giant lie that blocks us as a Body from being obedient to God. Thou shalt not lie. Remember that one? It's unlikely that He's going to pour out His power on a Church that is doing some good stuff, but also holding to one Great Lie - that is, "Look at us, we're Holy." -- when we're not and everybody knows it. If we're going to see revival or repentance or restoration or whatever is coming, it's not going to come until the Lie gets crushed and then washed out of the way.

Now, I want more than anything for us to be able to say, "Look at us, we're Holy." Please don't misunderstand. But when we do, it will be in gratitude and humility and worship for having God's help and provision to help us get there. And appreciation for Him giving us time to do it, instead of wiping us off the map like we deserve.

I'm going to try to point the way to Jesus all the time. The things He cared about are the very same things that today's liberal people seem to have a heart for - but that the church is ignoring. I'm not sure when we gave us this "high ground," but I'm sick and tired of it. It was Jesus that STARTED most of these things! Some of them were not even present on the planet before Jesus spoke of them!

Jesus came preaching peace with our enemies. He had a HUGE heart for children, especially those suffering. He cared about human justice and treatment of workers and equal protection. He empowered women in a male dominated culture. He cared about the environment. He spent time with people in "recovery" and addictive behavior - even criminals. He understood the needs of the handicapped. He ate organic foods (well, OK, they pretty much all did). He recycled and didn't waste resources. He only used ecologically sound transportation methods. He spoke harshly of anyone abusing or mistreating another person - particularly those in most need. He talked over and over about money and the important of helping the poor and the need for the rich to assume a greater role in that. (Read more on the "Was Jesus a Liberal" page.)

Anyway, the Apostle Paul spoke this, "First to those in Damascus, then to those in Jerusalem and in all Judea, and to the Gentiles also, I preached that they should repent and turn to God and prove their repentance by their deeds." (Acts 26:20) I had God in me before, but this is the time for me to repent, to take my focus off of Man and turn to God in full and to prove my repentance by my deeds. First, I personally have to change, then maybe other folks will get the hint.

But I'm not saying I'm perfect or anything. I'm going to stumble and I might screw this up. War against darkness means risk, especially the more attention you get. But whatever this becomes, I'm not taking credit for any of it. Pride is what got us into this mess! Shoot, I hardly see how I can take credit anyway, none of this was even my idea! I'm just doing as I'm told.

So that's the plan. If you still don't see why, read the next few letters. Maybe that will help.

(Now a few emails received from people that read the Apology to the World)

Jeff's "Apology To The Church"

Doug,

I hope that you will read this and not just delete it. I read your apology to the world for what the church has done to Jesus and his message of salvation. This is **my** apology to you and the church for trying to get inside and be a Christian.

First I have to tell about me so you can understand why I'm apologizing.

I grew up in a dysfunctional home with a alcoholic abusive father and a mother who was so abused and broken in spirit there was no protecting her children from him. I and my four sisters were verbally abused and sexually abused and physically abused at the hands of this man from the time we were born. My dad taught me how to abuse people and how to steal from anyone you could. He taught me swear and to cheat and to lie and to beat people up when you were angry. I found nothing wrong with these teachings as this man was my father and as a young boy he was naturally my guidance and my hero as I knew nothing else about being a person then what I was taught by my father. My father had destroyed all of my confidence and self esteem before I was two years old as I read it in a diary that my mother had kept hidden from him about her children. He had instilled in me that I was a useless waste of skin who would never amount to anything in this life and when I started to act out in school my teachers began to tell me the exact same thing. I sometimes wondered if there was a God or not as in those days when I was in grade school we still said the Lord's prayer in the mornings. If there was a God I sure wasn't given a very good life. My mom eventually ran away and left us there with him and things only got worse.

11

That set me on a course for a life of no meaning and a life of total hopelessness. A life where I was confident in only one thing, that I would never amount to anything so why should I even try. I had always been in trouble in school, but I started to get into real trouble when I eleven years old. I began stealing cars and doing break and enters as I wanted to out do my father and make him finally be proud of me for something. After all I had watched him steal since I was a small child.

I finally realized that my father was actually a coward when I saw him mouthing off in a bar and I guy beat him senseless while he laid on the ground covering his head while crying. I said to myself that "I would be no coward and then he would be proud of me so I set out to settle things with my fists and I would be afraid of no one. I began to go in and out of jail regularly and my life had only one meaning. To hate the world and all the people in it! I had never had a good relationship with any decent person in this world. I only knew criminals and abusive people who only tried to take from you what you had. When I was in jail for a one year sentence at age eighteen, I read the book The Late Great Planet Earth, by Hal Lindsay and it gave me an understanding of Bible prophecy and a good teaching for what to watch for as they unfolded and maybe, just maybe there was a God. I could not understand how this life could be so miserable and have just simply death at the end of it. I got my first handgun when I was twenty and I just got worse as life went on. I still spent the next six years in and out of prison and hating the world and everyone in it. I felt I had earned that right.

I found myself in prison at age twenty four and I began to get very depressed in this hopeless life. I prayed to Jesus a prayer. I simply said, "Jesus if you are real and you are there, I don't really want to die but I don't want to live like this anymore". Then I put a noose made out of a bed sheet around my neck and hung myself from the bars of my solitary confinement cell. Everything went black.

I went to the hospital in a coma which the doctors told my mom that I would never wake up from. They told her that it was a miracle that I was even alive and that I would lay in this vegetative state and that she should expect for me to soon die. The doctors were shocked to see me wake up from this coma. I was sent back to prison for the remainder of my sentence and slowly got better and my headache that lasted for months finally went away. The nurse in prison told me the story of how the guards found me hanging and they left me hanging there till they went and got her. It was at that point when she got there five minutes later that I was cut down with no signs of life whatsoever. The nurse got the defibrillator and shocked my heart five times with no response at all. The guards said to give up as I was obviously dead and she turned off the machine and looked at the clock to check the time of death. She turned back to see that the light for the defibrillator was on and it was ready to go again. She mentioned that she thought she had turned that off and tried one more shock just because it was ready to go. On the sixth try she shocked my heart and got a faint pulse. I was rushed to the hospital and put into intensive care where I remained in a coma till to everyones surprise I woke up from it. She said she was amazed because I was already getting cold.

This nurse kept asking me what did I see as she had never seen anyone who was dead for so long come back from it and she knew about near death experiences and wanted for me to tell her something about the other side. I saw nothing. I remembered nothing. She told me that I shouldn't even be alive and the fact that I could walk and talk was a miracle that she had never seen before. I vowed that when I got out of prison I would never go back. And I never did. The Bible says angels will encamp around those who will obtain salvation. This is true.

After I was later paroled from prison, I got my first real job at twenty six years old. I met a lady there and we began to live together for the next six years before we got married and my life got very stable. She had a grandmother who was ninety four years old and could no longer look after herself and she asked if we could take her in so she didn't have to go to a nursing home. We took her in willingly and gave her love and a good home. she was a church going lady and I suddenly found myself taking her to church on Sundays and Wednesday evenings. Her pastor used to pick her up and take her to church until she ran out of money to give them. The pastor and his wife would pick her up and take her to church. It seemed that my wifes grandmother was buying them things that they desperately needed like a $6,000.00 fur coat and a brand new $20,000.00 Chrysler Lebaron. They had convinced her that the Lord had said they needed these things. She gave them many more gifts that they said the Lord said she should give them, far too many to mention. She was a widower who really had nothing and saved her pension checks for thirty years. Her last $3,000.00 she gave to the pastor for his trip to Israel as he said he couldn't afford to go and he really wanted to go. This pastor and his wife lived in the most affluent neighborhood we had in the city in which we lived, in a house that could be described as a mansion. When the pastor found out that she no longer had any money he called her a burden and refused to pick her up for church any longer. That is when my wife and I began to take her. When people in her church found out that we weren't Christians yet they basically avoided us and never bothered to tell us about Jesus. When her church friends would come over to our house to visit her they would treat us badly because we weren't 'saved' and again no one told us about Jesus. I used to listen to this old grandmother pray for us before bed and she would always go off in a strange language that she never even understood, but I knew that there was something strange going on in her room at night during her prayers. She could no longer read her bible so she gave it to me one day and asked me to read it. I really wasn't interested in reading it after all the crap we seen happen to her and to us in her church. She died a year later. We vowed to never enter a church again.

I was still watching the prophecies that I read about in The Late Great Planet Earth, becoming fulfilled and it was

shocking to see and I began to realize that God could possibly be real. I began to study her old bible with a passion and began telling people about the prophecies and that it must mean that God is real. This went on for the next fourteen years and I got really good at associating prophecies with modern news events and using them to reach people for God. My mom and two of my sisters gave their hearts to the Lord because of these truths and are now deeply involved in their churches. Other people have become Christians when they had seen the truth in the bible of who created us and why. In a world of aliens and evolution some people just need a little truth. In the year 2002 we had a friend from where my wife worked and her husband over for the afternoon and she mentioned something about prophecy and we just spent the afternoon talking about bible prophecies.

This lady's husband was a lot like me, tough and rough around the edges, he liked drugs and drinking and had been in trouble in the past. He was strangely silent as I talked to his wife about these prophecies all afternoon. After they had left I said to my wife that we would never see him again because I didn't think he liked hearing about that stuff. I was shocked to answer the knock on the door four months later to see that it was him and he had a tape that he wanted us to see. He had given his heart to the Lord Jesus and it was a tape of his baptism and he wanted to share with us the life changes that he had gone through in the last four months. He told us that his wife and her mother were tying to get through to him but he would not receive any of it as it didn't make sense to him. He said to hear it from me was shocking as he knew my reputation for not taking any crap from anyone. We were shocked and something happened to me that day. I was jealous! I had seen this many times before when people learned about prophecy as it was proof that God existed. It was evidence for eternal life. Evidence for eternal damnation. Evidence for Jesus! I was jealous of his being baptised and I suddenly wanted to learn more about Jesus rather then just prophecies. I had suddenly felt empty, where he had knew life.

My wife and I vowed to never enter a church again after what we saw happen to her grandmother. If that was what Gods people were like we could do without them. I felt wrong after this meeting with that man who was changed by Jesus. I went into the bible with a vengeance and learned more about Jesus. Who he was and why he came here. I read about the gift of tongues and remembered my wifes grandmothers gift of tongues as she prayed for us because we took her in after her pastor took her for everything she had in this world. We went to a church that we heard was the best in the city and I was baptised in the water and I wanted to serve the Lord with everything I had to offer. Which I would soon find out, wasn't much.

Being that I grew up extremely poor I had no music talents to offer. There were no music lessons for me. I had never known a church or any teachings so again I had none of that to offer. I had tattoos and I was too rough around the edges to be accepted to help in any way. I was an ex con and the people didn't like that at all. They found out because there was a cop in the congregation who knew me. Why was a guy like me going to their church? I had gotten rid of my hate the world attitude prior to this and I saw a remarkable change come over me that was shocking! I could actually love people, but there was no acceptance for me there. I made the mistake of speaking of the bibles many prophecies that lead me to get saved in the first place and the people sure didn't like hearing about those! It was like they didn't believe in them. I made the mistake of trying to get people involved in leaving the church to go see people in the street and minister to them as that is what I got from the bible - we were supposed to make disciples out of everyone. Maybe I read it wrong, but to sit in a church with the doors open but not to invite anyone in seemed wrong to me. I made the mistake of trying to get people to learn more about prophecies so they could use them to reach their unsaved friends and family and co workers about the truth of God. It had worked for me in the past and I thought it was fairly effective as most people were turned off of Christianity because of things they had seen and experienced. Prophecy was the proof God gave us as to his existence. When I tried to talk to the head pastor about prophecies and how we could maybe use them to reach the lost souls, he called me preoccupied with that stuff and I didn't know what I was talking about. He wouldn't talk to me after that. I guess he didn't like me for trying to change things.

This is where I must apologize to you people in the church. I'm sorry. I apologize for thinking I had something to offer in your programs. After all you claim to try to help the depressed people with their problems and yet I know what it is like to put a rope around my neck and try to die and end the suffering. How many of you people can claim that? I heard you call the depressed people 'drainers'. They would drain you from hearing about their problems. Jesus wanted you to help them. I apologize for being too zealous in a place of complacency. I apologize for trying to get people to reach the lost souls around them. I apologize for trying to make you understand things about prophecy that you should know as being Gods people, tools you should be using to reach the lost. I apologize for going to prison in the first place but with my upbringing I really had no other choice. Most of you people were raised in a church setting and you weren't shown the things I was shown. You were taught values and different lessons than I was taught. You were encouraged where I was only discouraged. I was taught and shown hatred while you were shown love. I was taught anger and resentment and alcohol abuse and drug abuse. I apologize for trying to fit into your world when I clearly wasn't welcome into it.

I'm sorry.

I now sit alone with my family, afraid to go to a church. I lost all my friends when I got into Jesus. I couldn't make any church friends as I clearly wasn't their kind. I apologize to you for trying to be accepted for who I was rather than who you wanted in your world. I am thankful that Jesus accepted me for who I am rather than for who he wanted me to be. He will change me. I know why Jesus was always mad at the religious people, as I now find myself mad at them too. I now live again in a world of bitterness that I had at one time left behind me. I have actually had thoughts of suicide again since trying to fit into the church and being rejected. Bad feelings that have come back since being rejected by the church people. I only think of Jesus and his rejection by the very people he came to save and it makes it easier to understand. He never rejected the dying thief on the cross beside him. he never rejected the prostitute at the well. He never rejected anyone for their sins, he welcomed them with open arms and love and grace. I thought we were all supposed to be like him. I thought we were supposed to welcome the lost with compassion and love rather than judgement and condemnation. I thought we were supposed to believe the bible as the true word of God and not just pick out the things that we want to believe in.

Prophecy is a great tool to use to reach the lost in our world of reincarnation and evolution and Buddha and all the other false religions that we have. If Christians were half as zealous as Muslims are, this world would be a wonderful place and far fewer people would wind up in hell.

I apologize for thinking I had something to offer. I apologize for trying to make changes in your world. What do I know? After all I'm not as experienced as you guys are in this thing. But I sure was zealous and willing to learn. I'm now rejected and alone and in what seems like a prison, again! Thanks, and I'm sorry.

Jeff

Are you on your knees yet?!

Please hear me. If you are part of a congregation - or even a denomination - that has ever, EVER acted like this toward ANYONE, their blood is on YOUR head! Even if you're not the "pastor" - you helped build it and sustain it by your financial or physical support. If we're One Body and ANY part of the Body is in pain, shouldn't we ALL be hurting?! Why aren't we? Why aren't YOU? Why aren't you screaming for change? What is it going to take?

How many like Jeff are going to surface on Judgement Day and testify against you (and me)? Are you really so sure that Jesus is going to overlook all the testimony of

the people you've hurt just because you went down the aisle once and repeated a little prayer? If you LOVE HIM, you'll OBEY HIM! And He said to leave the 99 and go get the one lost sheep. And we're NOT doing it. In fact, it's the VERY LAST thing we're doing! And if one of the lost sheep happens to show up in "church" on their own – we THROW THEM OUT!!

Something is VERY, VERY wrong. It's got to stop NOW. We're running out of time.

Doug

Email from Sandie -
Can a simple apology really lift oppressions?

Just want to let you'all know -- I gave a copy of the "Apology" to a friend about a week ago. She has been enslaved to panic attacks for many many years. She hasn't even been able drive alone. She was very interested in what she read in "Apology" as she has dreadfully abused by the "system". She has been trodden on and made to feel like a nobody. Today she phoned and said that because of what she read, she decided to take a step in faith - guess what?? She drove, alone, by herself. OK OK it was half a kilometre but that is a giant step for her after so many years. "Apology" is bearing fruit -- it has given courage to someone and she is now looking forward to a complete release and recovery. Isn't Jesus wonderful?? Thank you again

Doug, for sending out such a humble and sincere message.

Sandie

Email from Brent -
Forgiveness comes AFTER confession

Dear Doug,

It is with a broken heart that I confess to you and any other that will hear my words, that I am one of the wrongdoers in the world. Sadness fills my heart when I consider the ways I offend the world with my hypocracy, not the world only, but The Lord Jesus Christ especially. Some of the things that I do and say I dare not mention even. Your words have given me a strong reminder of those things that really matter most, such as Integrity, HONOR TO GOD and love for TRUTH. Mercy is my plead. The shed blood of Calvary is my need. It would be a real blessing to hear of others that can say that they too, know the truth and want to walk in it. If there really is any good in me, it can only be Jesus in me. If there be any hope for me, it is in forgiveness.

Brent

Email from David and Debra -
Reaching the oppressed

Dear Brother Doug:

Just read your letter *{Apology}*. Three years ago, I was a Care pastor/ Life leader at a large Church. I thought I was doing good, living a Christian life. I had a good life, I had all I needed. Boy was I wrong! God called me to open a Mission here in Pell City, Alabama. My wife Debra and I had just the money to pay the rent, and cover the cost for one month. That was Oct. 28th, 2002. The Mission offers food, clothes, shoe, addiction programs, Bread Ministry, park and street ministries, community Bible studies and Sat. night services. Through Christ & prayer we believe that oppression can be overcome! In the last year and a half we have seen God free many people. It is AWESOME what God can and will do if we just let Him use us to help others! This is where most Churches are failing. They have forgotten the unchurched and yes even the oppressed churched.

Look around you. Someone needs help. Reach out to them, by blessing others, you will be blessed. Open your Heart and let the Holy Spirit work.

May God bless you, your family and ministry with mighty blessings now and always. Amen, Amen.

David

Brother Perry,

Amen. It's a blessing to learn of another brother who has come to terms with reality. I really feel like passing this along to my pastor dad, religious mom and other relatives and friends, and people I worked with at a denominational headquarters (I ran away from there)...but it's just like Christ said about how men come to the Father because He draws them. I don't think they are ready. I can't throw pearls before swine - have done that before to no avail. They seem to just become more determined to keep doing what they are doing. It's tough sitting by and watching the madness.

But, thanks for taking the initiative to put your revelation in words and present it to others. People in the world know who are hungry for God, those He is drawing, will recognize it if we have something they need. Nobody fools anybody in that regard...at least when we're talking genuine hunger and genuine Christians. I feel for all of the people who have been coerced/scared into saying a little prayer to receive Christ when they were not truly repentant. And I feel for those who were serious about accepting God, but then were led astray by false believers who were in it for themselves. Christ spoke about that too - very heavy.

Anyway, God bless you brother as you begin to live in the life, peace and rest that He intended.

J

Your letter was worth reading. My kids want no part of churchianity...and truthfully, neither do i. The fellowship or strengthening of one another's lives seems to be the closest to Christ's direction. But every time i hear of another program, i want to vomit.

Where are the people who will just open their homes and their hearts? Who want to speak of nothing but Jesus and the Kingdom...who do what He does, and say what He says....

I thank the Lord for every point of reality in the midst of pain, but it has been pain mostly of my own making, and i need my Savior.

Again, thank you,

Lee

I join you in "sorry." I forwarded your email to the elders of our church and to friends and family. I want to agree with you in prayer that God is merciful toward us all if we repent. I too have been sickened and defrauded in many instances where I have put my trust in leadership whose prime purpose was to build his/her own kingdom. But, I am reminded of when the disciples ran to Jesus to tell them that (another) Simon was preaching in the name of Jesus. Jesus' response was, in a word, "Let him alone, the main thing is that he is preaching the gospel." So, I trust that if and when the gospel comes/came forth that it reached many. We have all been a disappointment to others in the way we have lived our lives while representing the Lord; I truly repent. I pray we will have wisdom and integrity in the truest form which is in the form of Jesus. I attend a financially lean little church in the Hills of Texas and God is doing miraculous things in our midst; mostly because many are praying and desiring the sincere meat of the Word and trust everything to Him as we grow in faith and from glory to glory.

God Bless.

B.J.

Hi Doug

I am in agreement with your letter. I have told my children not to judge Christ by Christians. There have been recently some exceptions to that rule.

Another dissatisfied follower

Andrea

THANK YOU, THANK YOU, THANK YOU! So many others feel the same way and we have been "crucified" by the "church folk." I once had a Pastor who bragged on being like Paul of the New Testament, yet what he failed to realize was that he never had a "road to Damascus" experience, therefore his actions reflected more of Saul who killed Christians and honestly believed he was doing God a favor. Bless you for your stand. I too am sorry for what the Church has done to sinners... namely - kept them away from Christ who truly loves them!

Tina

QUOTE: "If you look at the world you'll be distressed, if you look within you'll be depressed, but if you look at Christ, you'll be at rest." Corrie Ten Boom

I just read your wonderful, beautiful gutsy letter to whom it may concern. That is the only way to be like Jesus! We have to live it. We are human imperfect beings, but one person at a time we can change things.

God Bless,

Linda

Doug Perry, thank you for the honesty in this message. I agree with you totally. Jesus, (Yahshua Messiah) was not like most people sitting in the pews and attending "Church" on Sunday, he was love and loved the unpriviledged. He would not and does not approve of what the "church" has become today. Again, thank you. Your sister in Jesus,

Doug.............Just received and read your article, "An Apology to the World". I can't tell you how much I appreciate this. I started an article some time ago of the same title but couldn't keep the bitterness and resentment out of it......so it still sits as an unfinished draft. I thank you soooo much for your gentleness and kindness and much needed expression of apology to a world in dire need that has become confused by religiosity and churchianity which poses falsely under the banner of Christ. Again, Thank you..........your brother,

Kelly

Thank you for this apology....I and my part of the Body of Christ join you in both the apology and repentance and commitment to be more like JESUS.......may HE fill us all daily with the fullness of HIMSELF and may we remain Faithful and True always abiding in HIM........CHRIST in us the HOPE of GLORY....this has got to be our story........Jan

Dear Doug,

Thank you for writing this, what a blessing to hear that we are not the only ones thinking that Jesus wouldn't really recognize "the Church" that we have made. A few years ago while in a service the Lord let me feel the deep sorrow that He feels when we play church. It was something that I've not talked about much but your letter very much expresses what He let me sense that evening. Well, thanks, keep on the same track and please know that if Jesus is truly Lord over us we will hear His voice and more and more of us will hear and more and more of us will come into that deep fellowship and love that He has caused us to grow into.

Blessings,

Dennis

I totally can understand where you are coming from. I was so turned off by my church because they did not follow scripture and were more worried about their building and programs than they were about my next meal as a single mother of 2 and no place to call home. Our church had several rental properties and I needed a place to stay....after paying my tithes faithfully...I thought they would allow me to rent. I was asked this question "if you had to choose between paying your car note and rent to the church which would you pay?" My reply was I would pay the car note since that is what got me to and from work.......needless to say I was not given the opportunity to rent. This is a huge church which does not need the income from the rental properties. I quit going there and have decided to pay my tithes to people who need the help, not the church. Thanks for putting it on my level......God Bless

JoAnne

I found your apology interesting. Thanks for penning it. I am forwarding it onto all my 'out-of-church' friends and to those 'unchurched' friends.

I wonder what would happen if I forwarded it onto TBN.

Jenny

{Hmmm. Well, I can tell you, Jenny, it's going to happen sooner or later! This is the word that needs to be spoken and I'm not going to stop till as many people as possible have heard it!}

Well that just totally rocked .... I've been apologizing to many folks over the last couple years myself ... in fact me and my hubby have been making a few waves since we decided to follow what Jesus said and did ... still walking it out though ... it's awesome ... HE rules!

Blessings Gayle

I agree with you 100%. I recently read "The Heavenly Man" and understand the China situation. How can we sit by everyday and see other humans starving or without water. What is wrong with us? Recently we repented also for the money we had spent on ourselves. Lord help us. We are with you all the way.

Janet

{I just CANNOT recommend a book more than "The Heavenly Man"! I know a certain crazy, radical, take-no-prisoners ex-skinhead revivalist that I sent a copy to who now thinks he's a big sissy compared to the Chinese Christians and Brother Yun! Order it at www.BackToJerusalem.com}

WOW!! I just found this web site. I was brought to tears. My heart leaped. I realized that what had happened to me and what I had been feeling and thinking about church and a reformation was on others minds and hearts also. I too have been ridiculed for leaving my church home of 16 years. I stayed until I could not (fight) it any longer....The spirit in me was being quenched and grieved. Once I realized that it was indeed God who was calling me out I had no choice but to go. I have had visions for years of different church...one with out walls...... I know that I as many others am waiting for God to open the door to the new thing. It is so close I know. I do get lonely for fellowship with other believers...but I am trusting in my Father and following his lead. God Bless you all.

Cecilia

---

yes! YES!

just recently have noticed all of this...big hubub at our church that made us leave(basically: group of us wanted MORE of God and the pastor and others said Nope.)...very sad (for them)...but i am happily on my journey now...

wow..how DO we unravel the hundreds of years worth of buildings and programs that replace Jesus, the Savior?

I want to be real...I want to do what the Father is doing...

I want my family to take the "Stop, look and Listen" break for Jesus and see where HE is going...and toss ALL aside and Follow Him.

thank you for your message!

Maryann

I just had to email you and tell you how much your article touched my heart!!!!! It is so true and we are all guilty!!!!! I have seen it at all of our local churches!!! Maybe that is why they are hurting so badly for new members.....I'm so sorry to say!!! I have forwarded your article to everyone on my email list in hopes that we can see the light and correct our ways!! God Bless You!!!

Joyce

Dear Mr. Perry,

I have just finished reading your letter, and all I can say is no truer words have ever been spoken, how horribly correct you are and how SAD it is to hear this truth. I do try to serve the Lord with my whole heart, but regretfully some of the things you said hit me to the core, I sat here in shame as I read your letter knowing that I too am guilty. In the days ahead I pray I too can become A person Jesus can honestly use.

Monica

I just had to email you and tell you how much your article touched my heart!!!!! It is so true and we are all guilty!!!!! I have seen it at all of our local churches!!! Maybe that is why they are hurting so badly for new members.....I'm so sorry to say!!! I have forwarded your article to everyone on my email list in hopes that we can see the light and correct our ways!! God Bless You!!! Joyce

---

thank you - i live in a retirement community - recently, i visited an old man - almost 86 - he is going in for serious surgery on wednesday - when i went to talk to him, he was afraid that he would not get to heaven. he said that he had turned down jobs that the "church" wanted him to do, etc. i asked him if he had a bible - he brought out an old bible - old but not very well read - i led him to Rom. 8:1 - no condemnation in Christ Jesus and on to rom. 10 - etc. he wrote the scriptures down and we have prayed. he is now at peace. i am angry that he had attended a "church" all his life and this was the end results. -- Fran

Great letter. It really stuck my heart. Please say a prayer for me for I am such a hypocrite.

Marc

Dear Doug, THANK YOU; I read your email which had been forwarded to me with great interest. As a new Christian of 10 months I found your email to be pretty much on the mark as to what I believe the church is like to day. Most of what I see are stale Christians or just plain thieves! Sorry but I to can be blunt too. I belong to a small church which is just beginning to come alive but they are still far from the mark. I have heard things said such as "your on fire now but hey that'll pass" you will get over it! What a joke!! I went back to working in a hotel as a Bouncer and was condemned by many Christians because a true Christian would not visit let alone work in a pub. Well I have had tremendous success in planting seeds, witnessing and leading people from the pub to Christ and I love it. I am also in the early stages of starting a ministry called aimed at Released Prisoners but to eventually cater for those 6 needs outlined in Mt 25 within the greater community. I was so please to see that there is a change of heart coming and you were brave enough to lead the way and put it out there for the world to read, Bless you my friend. I say thank you again for I know I am still far from perfect but do not wish to belong and fit in with that unhealthy view of Christians that much of the unreached public has. Thank You and God Bless, Graham

---

Email From Jim - Asking Hard Questions Will Get You Into Trouble!

Hello Doug,

I think you are exactly right on target with your comments. I marvel at how people spend money on themselves for exceedingly foolish things. Right now we are in the middle of the "Christmas Shopping Season". Frankly, I think we ought to take Christ *out* of Christmas and name the it for what it really is - "National Commerce Day".

I can really relate to your points in your article. I grew up in the Catholic church and right now there is a wave of church closings due to a shortage of priests. So what does the headquarters do? They close two churches and build a brand new multi-million dollar one. The church my parents attend is going to be merging with a smaller one. It would be easy for them to put an addition on the larger church to house everyone with minimal cost. But no - they will be building a huge new one four miles down the road.

When I first became a Christian, God took me on a circular route. I joined the Worldwide Church of God (which is the church Herbert Armstrong started). We paid one tithe on our gross income to meet the church's needs, then a second tithe to keep the Feast of Tabernacles (with the excess cash donated to the church), and every third year there was a third tithe for the widows and poor. I marvel at how the money (peak income for the church was something like $180,000,000 in one year) was just squandered mindlessly. I would hate to be some of the leaders of the church on Judgment Day. They will have some exceedingly hard questions to answer.

In all fairness, the WCG has undergone some serious doctrinal reforms in the past ten years and are now considered to be mainstream. Yet I still see them spending money to do evangelization but I don't see any results. If a person had to measure the spiritual "rate of return" on their financial investment - it might even be negative.

I felt a need to give my support to something that could use it better. The past few years I have been helping to support the local CSN radio station. (It is affiliated with Calvary Chapel). It seemed far better to support someone preaching the word of God chapter by chapter, verse by verse than to support the ideas of man. Yet even here, I wondered how many people were actually listening to the station. It is an excellent means of teaching those already in the faith, but how many new people is it reaching?

So then I started looking to support individuals who I know have needs. There is an elderly gentleman from our church who was having financial problems. Years ago he was almost killed when a drunk driver slammed into his car early one morning when he was going to work. It was very hard for him to work after that. They sold their farm to support themselves. It is amazing to me that for all the money the church headquarters collects, that they are unable to help people like these.

I am really convicted of the value of supporting groups like Gospel for Asia. I have heard of them in the past, but until recently, I have not looked into them. If a person would give 10% of their income to GFA for the purpose of buying Bibles and gospels and other appropriate materials to reach the lost - it staggers the imagination what they might be able to do with it. Even if each one of their missionaries would only convert a few people and they would start just one small church - that is an exceedingly more fruitful way to promote Gods' Kingdom than by giving to the organizations I have in the past. *{www.GFA.org}*

It is amazing to me how big churches spend their money. The most prominent mega-church in our area is Bayside Christian Fellowship in Green Bay, WI. I went to their services once. They have an auditorium that can seat 1200 people. It is very nice inside with TV cameras and projection screens to see the musicians up close while they perform, etc. One of the big things the pastor was talking about was a building project. Seems that they are pretty full on their two services on Sunday morning. Being dumb, I asked the foolish question of why they just didn't have a third service instead of paying millions to do an addition. I guess that was a dumb question. Also when I was there, they were praying for five people who were going to a foreign country for two weeks to do mission work. It just didn't make sense to me. For what it would cost to fly these people half-way around the world - for two weeks - to do what? They didn't know the language.

I would just like to encourage you to continue your website. There are people like me out here who do read it and are saying - "Right On". It is surprising to me that God has been patient with our country as long as He has. We certainly are not doing what we ought to be doing. I will forward your website to our pastor and talk to him about it. -- Jim

Email From Sandie -
Out of "Church" and Growing Like Crazy

Dear Doug Perry,

Thank you SO much for expressing my frustration with the church. This is why I left the "system" almost three years ago. The words did not match the deeds, there was no love or reaching out to those that needed to be reached, there was no compassion for those who were suffering. It was just one big comfort zone; a happy "bless-me" club, very much a clique -- and I did not fit in. My heart ached to see the hands of Jesus (through us) reaching out to the community around us instead of sitting on chairs for hours and hours, or dancing around having a "good" time instead of giving some Jesus joy to those that needed to be uplifted. The church seems to have become about "self" not Jesus. It speaks of prosperity (money). Financially I have very little, but consider myself prosperous because of what I have in God. I wouldn't swop my relationship with Him for all the money in the world. He is my treasure. He is the most precious gem I have ever gained -- and HE did it all -- not me.

He brought me to Himself in a most dynamic way when I was alone in my own home and since then I have followed Him for 17 years. The church taught me not to give to others but to itself and it seems so wrong. I met with more animosity and dislike in the church system than I ever did when I was " in the world". I was their worship leader, their only worship leader, yet when I contracted pneumonia and was sick at home for almost a year nobody phoned to see how I was or visited me. I was not resentful - I just could not understand why they were so angry. I did not ask to be ill. In retrospect I see that it was God's way of getting me out of there. The pastor is still angry with me. I never went back when I recovered. As there is no other English speaking church near me I have stayed at home and kept close to my Lord through His Word, His music, tapes and books. I have discovered a whole new perspective of God and it is nothing like that which is preached on a Sunday from a pulpit. I have discovered that He loves me just as I am, not as people want me to be. I have discovered that I am truly unique, that He made me that way for His glorious purpose. I believe that He is gently urging me into that purpose every day of my life until I go to be with Him forever.

I have discovered that I will not go to Hell just because I slip up with a bad word now and again, because that is the "old man" in me that HE is uncovering in me so that HE can get it out of me -- and that I don't have to have people shouting in my face trying to "deliver" me. I have discovered that He is VERY gentle with the way He sets me free from stuff that binds me. AND -- I have discovered that His love is so VAST and beautiful and compassionate and understanding. That is the most precious thing - that He understands me, that He knows me inside and out and still loves me in spite of myself. I never learnt that when I was in the church. I have discovered that He lets me know when He disapproves of something, and He does it in such a loving way. AND -- I have found that He leads me where He wants me to be in a much clearer way than I experienced when the "church" had its finger in my face.

I know of quite a few people like me who are "out-of-the-system" but love God so much. They are sincere, warm and loving - totally different to what I personally experienced in the church "system". I believe that God has a special plan for us if we would only stop, and listen. I believe that He is going to direct us into His path and His way of loving and giving. I am no longer worried about what people think - I am happy to go wherever my Lord takes me and do whatever He wants me to do. I am no longer feeling condemned because I do not go to "church". Wouldn't it be great to see the walls come down and the church in the streets just as Jesus was -- touching lives, changing lives, loving others just as God loves us..... IF only we could stop being so selfish and self-centered.

God bless you for having the courage to speak out what is in my heart, and the hearts of the friends God has given to me. With love in Jesus,

Sandie

Plea From A Missionary - Name Withheld Due To Her Humility

{response to "Apology to the World" that was forwarded to her by email}

I am so grateful that someone is saying this--at last! As a missionary wife, I came home from years on a pioneer field in great need of rest, good food, medical help and acceptance from people other than those who wanted to thrust me upon a platform to speak about, "Missions."

Couldn't I just once say something about how beastly hard it was trying to raise a child among poisonous snakes, scorpions, crocodiles, man-eating monitor lizards in the front yard, no friends for him, being his school teacher and Sunday School teacher and only companion, and a husband who was so consumed with, "the work," that he had no time for us? And I believed that was the proper way for him to be! I don't criticize this. I never talked about the millions of roaches in my house, about putting my child to sleep by saying, "Be very quiet, and you will hear the rats come into the house," Both my children are in Heaven now. I never spoke of things we had to eat, how thin and ill we all became, of sleeping in villages with bed bugs crawling all over us, with pigs in pens in the kitchen, of vomiting and diarrhea lasting up to a year, of being 80 miles from medical help, a very hard 80 miles. I never talked of any of this. I talked of people being saved, churches being established, elders being ordained, evangelists raised up by God who were faithfully serving Him without pay for years and years. But Oh, Lord, isn't there someone who will just care about me as a person? I tried to eat at all the feasts in my honor, taken from church to church and shown off; emotionally, I felt as if I were a ruin. I remember walking toward home for five hours at a time, sleeping in a village, and getting up again to do more walking, while having malaria. I didn't speak of this either. They wanted to hear about success, not bedbugs, not snakes, not scorpions and never rats in the house, and never discouragement and illness. At the meetings were I was featured as a speaker, I smiled and had my picture taken. Once, while in this country, I was given some black jam that someone had put up and stored in their basement for many years. "Missionaries can eat anything," I was told. Oh yes, and it was almost true. I thanked her for it, but didn't eat it.

Once, I told those on my mailing list that my husband was twice healed of very bad malaria attacks in which I feared for his life. The church gathered to pray, and my husband walked out of his room, cool and well. One church discontinued our support because they considered us Pentecostals from that time onward. I thought, sinfully, "Well if he had died, perhaps they would have remained friends with me and it would have suited their doctrine better."

I'm just glad someone is speaking out concerning the fat, wealthy church in America. But I might ask, "Is this really the true church? Is this all there is here? Are there none who are generous, unselfish, loving and have the Spirit of God in them? Is there no true church in this country? We have been looking for such a place for a long time.

I am unwell now, and could be said to be elderly and I don't do much beyond praying any more. My dear, whitehaired husband is still a missionary who wins souls, and tries to teach them and support these new lives in Christ, giving them Bibles and other materials, and corresponds with them. We think we have found a church where the pastor is a humble, intelligent man; the congregation is a mixed-race group, which I like. An intelligent, Black woman is the only adult Sunday School teacher, and yes, men sit in her class, gratefully appreciating her; the class is large. As a rule, we are unable to stay for that. My husband is still a tireless evangelist, but he has time for me now.

God bless you and may your tribe increase!

In Christ's love,

(A missionary)

+++

My Commentary on "Plea from a Missionary"

ARGGGHHHH!!!!

This could be my Mom! (Had she not died of cancer after we came back to the States.) I lived the missionary life as a kid, I understand this. I had to BEG this dear sweet warrior of God to let me publish this so you could see this. I couldn't have written anything as convicting!

Listen, you can't send out advance troops to do battle and expect them to succeed with no ammunition, no supplies and no backup. Read Judges 6-7. When Gideon's 300 went out to fight 150,000 Midianites with a torch in one hand and a trumpet in the other - the other 31,700 that couldn't hack it got to stay home, but they LEFT ALL THEIR STUFF BEHIND! So the 300 had enough provisions for 32,000!! THAT is how GOD does battle! Those willing to go lay down their lives for Jesus should have 100 TIMES their own needs so that they can feed any who are hungry and give drink to any who are thirsty.

AND STOP MAKING THEM COME HOME AND DO SLIDE SHOWS!!! LOVE ON THEM WITH EVERYTHING IN YOU AND BE GRATEFUL GOD DIDN'T SEND *YOU* TO DO IT!! And if He DID send you to do it and you're trying to hide from it - then you owe these people TWICE as much!!

STOP USING THEM TO MAKE YOUR STATS LOOK GOOD AND EASE YOUR CONSCIENCE! These are WARRIORS! Treat them like it and give them the provisions they need without making them stop everything and come entertain YOU every four years!

Take the Bentleys and Mercedes away from the fat cat pastors, sell them off and give the money to the front line warriors that are IMMUNE to the love of money! If you're willing to take your kids to go live in a jungle a five hour walk from help - I'm just SURE I can trust you with money! If you have a million dollar house, I gotta wonder.

We just don't have time for this anymore!! Who is running this war?!

Doug

Musical Interlude -
Feel free to sing along

This is my commandment that you love one another,
that your joy may be full.

This is my commandment that you love one another,
that your joy may be full.

That your joy may be full.
That your joy may be full.

This is my commandment that you love one another,
that your joy may be full.

Very good. It's really all very simple, isn't it?

Now ...

STOP teaching this song to your kids
if you're <u>not</u> going to live it!!

You're just confusing them!!

NEGATIVE EMAILS FROM THE APOLOGY TO THE WORLD
(and some responses)

The very <u>first</u> serious flaming mad email! - of many to come.

Shalom. Barukh atah Ha-shem, Eloykaynu, melekh ha-olam.

Speak for yourself. I know no true Christians who do any of those things. I can only wonder what kind of Christians you know. Try looking at the traditional churches and not wacky Protestant churches with no roots or real beliefs. I don't know what your motivation is, but if you are trying to damage the name of Christianity, you are succeeding. If you are attempting to be satirical, you are failing dismally.

Don't judge all Christians by yourself and your circle of acquaintances. What you say is a total insult to the majority of Christians and only true of prosperity doctrine sects. It is the worst drivel I have ever read, even from Protestant fundamentalists. If you seriously imagine that anyone is going to be interested enough to read all that verbiage, you are grossly flattering yourself. No non-Christian is, and not many Christians.

I certainly will not be coming to hear you speak, if your spoken message is as grovelling as your email, which I think is likely to turn people right off Christianity.

Just who do you think you are, to put down millions of Christians and set yourself up as judge, the only person with any principles ? Your conceit is beyond belief. Humility is not a word with which you appear to be familiar.

And 'churchianity' is not a word; it is nonsense.

Anna

++

{MY RESPONSE}

Anna,

I WAS speaking for myself. It's MY apology.

Either we're ONE body or we're not. If we are, then we're failing miserably. There is no other way to look at it. Across the totality of what we call "Christianity" in the West there is negative growth and MUCH damage to many, many lives.

If you think YOUR sect is universally being effective and doing the right thing, then you stand accused of having separated off instead of trying to heal the Body. Even those doing the right thing should have put a stop to this sooner.

Put your head in the sand if you like, but there is unarguable statistical and demographic evidence that there is a massive movement AWAY from the churches across nearly all denominations. There are over 20,000,000 "wilderness Christians" in America that are worshiping God on their own because "church" is too toxic for them.

The time has come for someone to admit the truth. This is NOT the way Jesus wanted it. We've segmented ONE BODY up into thousands of denominations and sects. The "world" sees how messed up it is. It seems like the most honest thing is to just admit it. Then the healing can begin.

If what I have to say and my motivation for doing it is "of man" then it will surely fail. If it is "of God" then there is no stopping it. I guess you'll get to sit back and smugly watch to see what happens. Meanwhile, me and anybody else willing are going to go try to get people focused back on Jesus, instead of the man-made systems and structures we created without Him.   -   Doug

+++++++++++++++++++++++++++++

(MY SIDE COMMENTARY)

First, if somebody would like to translate the Hebrew for me, that'd be nice. Not my thing.

Second, WOOHOO!!!! The more angry they get, the more we're probably saying things that make them uncomfortable! Jesus said there would be

persecution. This is just the very, very start of it. There will be MUCH anger.

Third, see how "roots" are so important to her? Tradition, history, structure, etc. seems to impart legitimacy. The older the denomination, the more True? Hmmmm.

Can you see the hate for Protestants? The absolute sense that they are stupid rednecks that are mucking it up for the "real" religions?

Oh, PLUS - it's just bad logic. If nobody is going to read it, I can't hardly be causing any damage, now can I?

Another One - Unsigned

It's good to say what we aren't supposed to be, but where is the standard of what we ARE supposed to be. That is the mark of a true prophet!

Are we not doing anything right? Did Jesus Himself as well as Paul say that we were to get some reward from following Him? I think so!!!

Not everyone is CALLED to be a martyr in the sense of living destitute for the Kingdom. Big churches often are doing more than small churches. And sometimes you do have to look at the percentages as well as the intangible assets.

Most Christians are not living that much different from the world BECAUSE that IS the world they live in and that is HOW they reach others.

Can we do more? Always! Just like we can always pray more - so what is the standard.

I get tired of being put down by the self righteous who give no standards for me to say, "Maybe I am on the right track!"

The world is not just the poor guy on the street corner - we should help him, but the world is the world! And we are to reach it. There are a lot of ministry styles I like and many I don't. But guess what, when you take a poll, not every one's tastes and styles are the same. Don't factor that out.

Many are doing MUCH MORE than you are giving them credit for. Do we need to work on it? Sure! But change comes by His Spirit. Not by just another voice of authority that criticizes everyone else.

++++++++++++++++++++++++++++++++

{MY RESPONSE}

Hi,

First, that letter was to the "World" - NOT to the church. That was an APOLOGY, not purely a lecture on what the RIGHT thing is.

Second, that other stuff you're asking about is on the website and more is coming. Particularly see the Declaration of War and the Battle Plan.

This is a big problem, we're not going to fix it in one email, particularly an email that wasn't aimed at YOU.

Prophets don't consider individual cases. Hosea didn't say "just the bad ones are going into captivity". Everybody stands condemned, including the righteous remnant that should have been trying harder to stop the bleeding.

If we're ONE Body, then we need to look at our success or failure in those terms. We have sliced the body up into 33,000 sections. Necessary and complementary organs aren't talking to each other. Blood isn't flowing to the extremities. We're dying. There's no other conclusion.

Nobody is saying martyrs are to be destitute. Where'd you get that? We are to offer our bodies as living sacrifices, we are to be willing to crucify little pieces of ourselves everyday, we are to grow up into Him who is the Head, we are to pour ourselves out as a drink offering so that HE can be poured in. That's the nature of martyrdom. And EVERY SINGLE Christian should be willing to do so - that's our spiritual act of worship commensurate with the mercy He's shown us. It's all there in Romans 12. A person that says they are a Christian but that isn't willing to do so is saying that they aren't willing to BE like Christ, but are willing to use His name. They should be encouraged or else ignored - but never made a leader.

Take a look around the website before you dismiss it so easily. This is the word that needs to be spoken.

Doug

More Criticism – from Al

I read most of the articles on your web site today.

Have you ever asked yourself why you take up various causes? What is your true motive?

You will probably have to ask Jesus to explain to you, your real motives. It isn't what first leaps to your mind. If you get the real answer, it will be an awakening. It will be the first step in a long road to discover yourself. Something that is vital to a deeper relationship with God.

Almost all of your conclusions and opinions come from the mind of reason. They are superficial because they do not deal with the real forces that shape this world. Instead, the opinions are based upon human understanding.

John, in quoting Jesus, said that worship of God must be in spirit and truth. Don't gloss over the dynamics of that concept. What does it mean to worship in truth? (By the way, only John makes this quote.)

Al

+++++++++++++++++++++++++++++++

{MY RESPONSE}

Hi Al,

Now, please understand, I mean this in the most loving possible way.

HUH?

I have no intention of trying to "discover" myself! In fact, I don't even want there to be any of "myself" left. I turned it all over to God and said I'd do whatever He wanted and this is what I got. I'm just trying to be obedient every day.

If the arguments seem superficial it's because the people have been dumbed down so much that we require remedial education. It's not enough to just talk about the eternal struggle between good and evil that happens behind the scenes. People need to see the consequences of that warfare in the "natural". We can see the side effects of the warfare in the current pitiful state of the visible church (as a whole). I'm pointing out the damage caused in the natural by us having ignored the supernatural.

Other than that, I'm not even sure what you're trying to say. There's a difference between knowledge and wisdom. I'm trying to inflict maximum damage on the enemy in as short a time as possible. That's going to require rallying those already prepared and training those who are willing but green. That requires wisdom. I'm a soldier following the battle plan as laid out by my Commander. I don't have time for too much thinking - that's what got us into this mess.

I just don't see it as being that complicated. Acknowledge Him, submit, beg to hear His voice as clear as you can, repent, hear what He wants and GO DO IT - then give Him alone the credit. It's all in the Lord's Prayer.

I am what I am because HE made me. I have ZERO desire to delve into the mystery that is "me". I just do as I'm told.   --- Doug

+++++++++++++++++++++++++++++

{AL'S RESPONSE}

Thanks for your reply. Unfortunately, it was what I had expected. But, I was hoping otherwise.

It is so sad that often those who believe they are doing something for the Lord, don't really understand the deception they are under. What's equally sad is that deception has many levels and it will justify itself.

Never are the deceived, so deceived, as when it involves religious matters!

Al

+++++++++++++++++++++++++++++

{MY SECOND RESPONSE}

Sorry, Al.

Gotta do what I gotta do. Either it's God talking to me or it's not. If it's of man it's gonna fail anyway and you can smugly watch me go down in flames. If it's of God, folks probably ought to think twice before fighting against it. Good advice from Gamaliel. (Acts 5:33-39)

Wish I could slow down to argue it all out with you, but I'm fighting a war here. I guess I'll just take my

chances at the final judgement. -- Doug

+++++++++++++++++++++++++++

(MY SIDE COMMENTARY)

Listen folks, this is the lie from the pit. "Figure yourself out. Find your inner purpose. What's your motivation? What makes you tick."

Most of this email I can't even make sense of. But I'm just NOT going to get suckered into it! We're to be a living sacrifice (Rom. 12). The SACRIFICE itself doesn't get to decide ANYTHING. The sacrifice lays there on the altar and GOD decides what to do with us. If we turn over everything, He will very quickly help us to: STOP CONFORMING TO THE WORLD, then He will transform us by the renewing of our minds, so that we can know HIS will and DO IT. That's all there is to it.

DON'T get suckered into these fights! YOUR personal "purpose" doesn't matter a flying fig. Find out what GOD wants and then DO IT. No more messing around with psychobabble.

Another Response - From Brian

While I understand your intentions, this kind of statement, no matter how true some facts may be, in the end, rarely brings about anything other then a mocking laugh from "the world". Also, even the best criticizers and challengers of churchianity within the church eventually tire, being isolated and considered fringe elements, hurt and bittered by the devil, and the church. I've seen person after person face this. Jesus challenged and provoked the religious status quo, but did not become critical of it. He rose to a higher purpose (to send the gospel to the gentiles, the world) and position (seated at the right hand)

My suggestion is that you take Christ's lead and become the model of non-churchianity and even come together with others that feel the same and start another church. Only new churches that embody the real Christ have an impact and help change individuals and churches.

While you may want to take the opportunity to preach back to me, I do hope you take some time to chronicle your positions and the perceived impact your having. Look at the impact over the next 10 or 20 years and then compare it to the word and see if your ministry had value. It will be real clear then.

Take Care

Brian

++++++++++++++++++++++++++++++++

{MY RESPONSE}

Thanks, Brian.

The fact that others have fought and lost is no excuse to stop fighting. The fact that I might not win is no excuse to stop fighting. The fact that there will always be someone somewhere mad at you is no excuse to stop fighting. The fact that the world might laugh at you is no excuse to stop fighting. You really honestly believe Jesus didn't criticize the religious status quo?! He called them murderous, hypocritical, greedy, self-indulgent, unclean, vipers, white-washed tombs of dead men's bones AND said they were all going to hell! (Matt. 23)

I don't want to start another church! I want people to fill themselves and the churches we already have with

JESUS. And not settle for anything less. What do you want for them?

Always good advice to journal and think back and see what impact we've had. I'd take you up on that – writing everything down for 10 or 20 years - but I'll be dead way before then. --- Doug

DECLARATION OF WAR AGAINST THE FORCES OF DARKNESS

Now, before you start thinking we're talking about YOU, this is about EVIL - not people. Sure, some people are stinkers, but we're to love people and we're to hate evil. The darkness from our sinful nature is in all of us. We're not any better, it's just Christ in us that helps us be redeemed. Anyway, this is about the BIG picture, not any specific person, organization, leader, etc.

No more. It ends now.

For too long we've ignored what was going on in the church. For too long we've sat out or even denied there was a war. We've been infiltrated. We've been co-opted. We've been dumbed down. We've had our greatest weapons ridiculed and demeaned until nobody wants them anymore. This is no kind of way to fight a war.

We've allowed ourselves to be fattened up and we've planted roots. We've been herded together in big groups like cattle and we bump around against each other making useless noises. Wolves have come in and we've welcomed them. We've accepted aid from the enemies of God. We've taken the enemy's advice about how to make war. We've hired consultants to show us how to be more like the world.

We've ignored our own King's plan. We've sent a pitiful few skirmishing parties out to do the work of missions for us and patronized them when they come home wounded and hungry. We've given all the ammunition to the supply clerks back home and deprived the infantry of what they needed to push back the darkness. Everything about what we're doing is upside down.

No more will we take on the names and philosophies of men to define and identify us. No more will we allow factions over secondary issues to divide us. We are to be OF Jesus and Him alone. Only He gets to put His brand on us. Only He gets to direct us. Only He is truth. This is war! Nothing else can be trusted. His is the unbreakable cypher. Pure, full, uncut Truth cannot be spoken by the enemy. Truth and Love are our uniform, our code, our defining characteristic. Only Truth and Love will suffice for battle against principalities and forces of darkness.

No more will we waste time on our own vain pleasures and indulgences. No more will we allow the egos and prides and traditions and philosophies of Man to divide us. We will love Truth and settle for nothing less. We will learn to sniff out and purge compromise and half-truths. We will force out of us every bad dark thing by being completely filled with the Bread of Life. We will be nourished by Truth. We will be armored by Truth. We will swing the Sword of Truth in big wide circles and pierce the hearts of anyone near. We will fight and not grow weary. We will charge forward and never retreat. Should one slip, others will lift him up. Should one fall, others will take his place.

No more. It ends now. There are those that are already equipped to fight and we will enlist them, organize them and send them back out to recruit more. We'll fight with love to awaken our brethren who are asleep and get them in fighting form. We will push back the darkness by speaking nothing but TRUTH. It is rare and precious - and only Jesus is the source. Every man-made thing will burn off in the fire. Only Jesus can be trusted.

As Gideon, we will lovingly restore our own altars first while the people are sleeping. Then we can rally a restored, awakened people to fight the forces of darkness. Those on the front lines that have proven themselves good and faithful servants and stewards of their talents will be provisioned with a hundred times their own needs so that they can feed the hungry and give drink to the thirsty as they see any need. We will pray and encourage and support them and recruit more. We will always strive to continue growing up into Jesus, who is the Head. In view of the great mercy shown us by Jesus Christ, we will offer our bodies as living sacrifices, holy and pleasing to God. We will stop conforming to the pattern of this world. We will be transformed by the renewing of our minds so that we will be able to test and approve what is God's good, pleasing and perfect will. Then we'll go and do it. **I Corinthians 14:8** - *"Again, if the trumpet make an uncertain sound, who will prepare for battle?"*

No more. It ends now. As clear as we can say it, this is war.

FELLOWSHIP OF THE MARTYRS
BATTLE PLAN

Acknowledge your complete needfulness for God and inability to reach Heaven and escape the consequences of sin on your own power. Repent of every sin. Acknowledge Jesus as the risen Son of God and beg Him to wipe you clean. Commit to Him that He will be Lord and Master and that He alone will direct you. Without any reservation or evasion, you must mean that you intend to seek Him and do as He leads - even if it means discomfort, abuse, sacrifice, change, suffering, separation or even death. Ask for the indwelling of the Holy Spirit in as great a measure as He is willing to give you. Don't seek gifts for the sake of gifts, seek God - and He'll decide on the gifts for you. Be willing to chase holiness - to strive and urge forward for it everyday. Go and sin no more.

If you mean that Christ is Lord, then you must mean that His Word is the final authority. Spend most of your time in praise and worship of God because He is holy. This is the most pure expression of our love - for this we were made. Seek out anybody else that is absolutely committed to doing as God directs and is willing to speak only Truth, even if it's hard. Spend time together praising God and seeking His face. Each of you be prepared to minister. Don't rely on a paid staff person to do it.

The ultimate source of Truth is God's Word. Learn to love it, take it everywhere, read it and ask the Holy Spirit to explain and teach you what you need. Practice speaking pure Truth with no hint of Man inserted. Test everything against the Word of God.

Hold onto the good, run from evil. Learn to have no love for any created thing that exceeds your love for the Creator. Work hard. Whatever you do, do it as if you are doing it for God. Pray that God will help you have as large a positive impact as possible. More than anything else, God wants to first restore His people and convert all the altars back to the worship of God. Pray for the churches.

Take big arm loads of Truth and begin feeding the hungry. Go out as missionaries to speak into the hearts of the people where God leads you. Always speak in love and humility, pointing the way to Christ alone. Remember, you are trying to save eternal souls - never focus even for a moment on the immediate, always on the eternal.

Find those who can also commit themselves fully to Christ and involve them in your fellowship. Praise God always for His use of you to save others. As your act of obedience, divert all available resources and assets only to those individuals and organizations most efficiently converting earthly treasure into heavenly treasure - that is, feeding the hungry, reaching the lost, caring for widows and orphans, supporting the Brethren in the hard places, equipping missionaries to push back the darkness - the same priorities that Christ has. Anyone that shows a "love of money" should be instantly suspect of being ensnared by the enemy and should be prayed for desperately - that is the root of much evil. God has already prepared many who are no longer susceptible to attack from that direction - find them and give them what they need.

Seek out other fellowships and submit to each other in love. Seek to support the members of your own fellowship as they go to serve or split off to start more fellowships. Seek unity through harmony. Don't get distracted for a single moment by secondary issues or debates. We don't want everybody singing the melody, we want everyone in harmony and singing the part written for them by God. We need all the pieces. None can be wasted. But be willing to rebuke as God directs, and forgive if they repent. Expect wolves, spies and infiltrators. Expect the enemy to be sneaky. This is war.

As you stay inside of Truth, get to know the will of God and use all your gifts and talents within His will, amazing things are likely to happen. Expect miracles. Beg to be filled with the empowering of the Holy Spirit and use what gifts He's given you. Stay filled by a constant focus on holiness and purity and praise. Then pray that God will enlarge you so you can hold more. Pray for the greater gifts - those that can do the most damage to the enemy.

Obey God only. Time is short - so don't waste any. Go in love - and never give in.

FELLOWSHIP OF THE MARTYRS
BATTLE PLAN
(Extended Version)

This is by no means a comprehensive list of verses related to each of these items. There are two purposes in doing this expanded version. One is to show that every single line is based on Scripture. The other is to provide a lesson plan that can be used as a study guide to work through each of these items. Whether individually, in small groups or as a larger church, these are the core fundamentals that should be foremost on our minds. We hope that this will bring value to you. As you find other verses that clearly apply to any of these lines, please email us and we'll add them.

We're building this together. Rediscovering the simplicity of God's Plan.

1. Acknowledge your complete needfulness for God and inability to reach Heaven and escape the consequences of sin on your own power.

Genesis 4:6-7; 2 Chronicles 7:14; Psalm 38; Proverbs 5:21-23; Proverbs 10:17; Proverbs 16:5-6; John 3:16; Romans 6:23; Romans 10:9-10; Ephesians 2:8; 1 John 1:9;

2. Repent of every sin.

Psalm 32:1-7; Psalm 51; Luke 13:3; Acts 17:30; 2 Corinthians 7:10; Rev.3:19

3. Acknowledge Jesus as the risen Son of God and beg Him to wipe you clean.

Psalm 119:94; Mark 10:32-34; John 1:29-34; Acts 22:16; Acts 26:23-24; Ephesians 5:26; 1 Corinthians 15:20; 1 Timothy 2:5; I John 4:9-10; Titus 3:5; Revelation 1:5;

4. Commit to Him that He will be Lord and Master and that He alone will direct you.

Proverbs 3:5; Matthew 22:37; 2 Corinthians 1:21-22;

5. Without any reservation or evasion, you must mean that you intend to seek Him and do as He leads – even if it means discomfort, abuse, sacrifice, change, suffering, separation or even death.

Psalm 4:5; Psalm 18; Romans 12; Matthew 10:32-33; Mark 10:29-31; Romans 8:18; Romans 1:17; Galatians 2:20; Galatians 6:14-15; Philippians 3:7-11; I John 5:3-5;

6. Ask for the indwelling of the Holy Spirit in as great a measure as He is willing to give you.

Luke 11:13; Acts 1:8; Ephesians 3:14-19; 1 John 5:14-15;

7. Don't seek gifts for the sake of gifts, seek God - and He'll decide on the gifts for you.

Psa 42:1-2; Rom 12; Matt. 6:33; 1 Corin. 12:7-11; James 1:5

8. Be willing to chase holiness - to strive and urge forward for it everyday. Go and sin no more.

Psalm 17:3-5; Psalm 39; Psalm 66:16-20; Psalm 119; Mark 9:42-49; Luke 17:1-3; Romans 6; Romans 8:1-17; Romans 12; 1 Corin 6:9-10; 2 Corin 13:11; Colossians 3:1-17; I John 5:18;

9. If you mean that Christ is Lord, then you must mean that His Word is the final authority.

John 1:1-4,14; John 8:32; John 14:21; John 14:6; Romans 3:4; Hebrews 4:12;

10. Spend most of your time in praise and worship of God because He is holy. This is the most pure expression of our love - for this we were made.

Exodus 4:31; Psalm 12:4; Psalm 29:1-2; Psalm 34:1-8; Psalm 47:1-2; Psalm 104:33-35, Psalm 103; Ps. 113:3;

11. Seek out anybody else that is absolutely committed to doing as God directs and is willing to speak only Truth, even if it's hard.

Ecclesiastes 4:9; Romans 12; I Corin. 5:9-13; I John 4:1-8;

12. Spend time together praising God and seeking His face.

Psalm 32:11; Matthew 6:33; Colossians 3:15-17;

13. Each of you be prepared to minister. Don't rely on a paid staff person to do it.

Luke 17-20-21; I Corinthians 14:26-33; Colossians 3:15-17;

14. The ultimate source of Truth is God's Word.

Deuteronomy 6:4-9; Psalm 119:105,130; Proverbs 30:5; Isaiah 40:8, 55:10-11; John 1:1,14; John 8:32; John 17:17; Romans 3:4; 2 Timothy 1:50; Rev.19:13;

15. Learn to love it, take it everywhere, read it and ask the Holy Spirit to explain and teach you what you need.

Deuteronomy 8:3; Psalm 119; Acts 20:35;

16. Practice speaking pure Truth with no hint of Man inserted.

Proverbs 10:19-21; Zechariah 8:16; Romans 12; I John 1:-10;

17. Test everything against the Word of God. Hold onto the good, run from evil.

John 5:39; Acts 17:11; Romans 12:9; 1 Corinthians 15:2; 1 Timothy 6:11; I Thessalonians 5:21-22; James 4:7;

18. Learn to have no love for any created thing that exceeds your love for the Creator.

Psalm 39:6; Matthew 6:24; Matthew 10:34-39;

19. Work hard. Whatever you do, do it as if you are doing it for God.

Colossians 3:23-25;

20. Pray that God will help you have as large a positive impact as possible.

1Chronicles 4:10; Colossians 4:2-4;

21. More than anything else, God wants to first restore His people and convert all the altars back to the worship of God.

Judges 6; 2 Chronicles 29 –31; Malachi 3:7;

22. Pray for the churches.

Ezekiel 22:30; John 17:9,20-21; Acts 6:4; Acts 12:5; 1 Thessalonians 5:16-18; 1 Thess. 5:25; James 5:13,16;

23. Take big arm loads of Truth and begin feeding the hungry.

Matt.10:27; Luke 9:60; John 14:6; Romans 12;

24. Go out as missionaries to speak into the hearts of the people where God leads you.

Matthew 28:19-20; Luke 10:1-9; Acts 1:8; I Corinthians 5:9-13;

25. Always speak in love and humility, pointing the way to Christ alone.

Luke 17:10; Luke 18:9-14; Luke 18:16-17; Luke 22:24-30; Colos. 3:15-17; Eph, 5:2; 1 Corin 13:1; 1 Corin 16:14;

26. Remember, you are trying to save eternal souls - never focus even for a moment on the immediate, always on the eternal.

Matthew 6:19-21; Luke 10:1-9; Romans 8:18-39;

27. Find those who can also commit themselves fully to Christ and involve them in your fellowship.

James 4:1-10

28. Praise God always for His use of you to save others.

Psalms 113:3

29. As your act of obedience, divert all available resources and assets only to those individuals and organizations most efficiently converting earthly treasure into heavenly treasure - that is, feeding the hungry, reaching the lost, caring for widows and orphans, supporting the Brethren in the hard places, equipping missionaries to push back the darkness - the same priorities that Christ has.

Matthew 6:19-21; Mark 10:21-31; Luke 16:9; Luke 18:22; Romans 12;

30. Anyone that shows a "love of money" should be instantly suspect of being ensnared by the enemy and should be prayed for desperately - that is the root of much evil.

Matthew 6:24; Luke 16:19-31; Luke 17:33; Luke 18:18-30; Luke 19:1-9; Luke 19:45-46; Luke 21:1-3; I Corinthians 5:9-13;

31. God has already prepared many who are no longer susceptible to attack from that direction - find them and give them what they need.

Luke 16:10-13; Luke 19:11-27; James 1:9-12; James 2:5-6; 2 Peter 2:1-3;

32. Seek out other fellowships and submit to each other in love.

Mark 9:50; Luke 17:3-4; 1Corinthians 16:14;

33. Seek to support the members of your own fellowship as they go to serve or split off to start more fellowships.

Matthew 9:35-38; Acts 4:32; Romans 12;

34. Seek unity through harmony. Don't get distracted for a single moment by secondary issues or debates.

Romans 12; Romans 14-15:13; Galatians 5:16-26; Ephesians 4:1-6, 13-16, 25; Philippians 2:2; 1 Corinthians 1:10; 2 Corinthians 6:15; 2 Corinthians 13:11; I Peter 3:8; I Timothy 6:20-21; James 5:9;

35. We don't want everybody singing the melody, we want everyone in harmony and singing the part written for them by God.

Romans 9:20-21; Romans 12; I Corinthians 11:18-19

36. We need all the pieces. None can be wasted.

John 17:4; Romans 12; 1 Corinthians 12:7-11; Ephesians 4:11-13; Philippians 1:6;

37. But be willing to rebuke as God directs, and forgive if they repent.

Luke 17:3-4; Romans 12; Galatians 6:1; Colossians 3:13;

38. Expect wolves and spies and infiltrators. Expect the enemy to be sneaky. This is war.

Proverbs 24:5-6; Proverbs 14:1-2; Matthew 15:8-9; Mark 13:1-13; Luke 20:20-26; Luke 20:45-47; John 15:18-21; Ephesians 6:10-18; 2 Corinthians 10:3-6; I Timothy 1:18-19; 2 Timothy 3:12;

39. As you stay inside of Truth, get to know the will of God and use all your gifts and talents within His will, amazing things are likely to happen.

Romans 12:2; 1Thess. 5:16-18; The whole book of Acts!

40. Expect miracles.

John 1:50; John 14:12-14; The whole book of Acts!

41. Beg to be filled with the empowering of the Holy Spirit and use what gifts He's given you.

Luke 11:13; Romans 8:11; Romans 12; I Corinthians 14:12;

42. Stay filled by a constant focus on holiness and purity and praise.

Genesis 4:6-7; Psalm 51; Psalm 113:3; Romans 8:4; Romans 8:6; 2 Corinthians 10:5;

43. Then pray that God will enlarge you so you can hold more.

Exodus 34:24; Deuteronomy 12:20; Deuteronomy 19:8; 1 Chronicles 4:10; 1 Chronicles 4:10, Isaiah 54:2, 2 Corin. 9:10;

44. Pray for the greater gifts - those that can do the most damage to the enemy.

1 Kings 3:9; I Corin. 13:27-21; I Corin. 14:1; I Corin. 14:12;

45. Obey God only.

Psalm 32:8-11; Isaiah 64:8; Matthew 4:10; John 14:21; Romans 6:22; 1 Corinthians 6:20;

46. Time is short -

Matthew 3:2; Matthew 24:36,42-44; Matthew 25:13; Luke 17:22-36; 2 Peter 3:10;

47. so don't waste any.

Ezekiel 3:17-21; Hebrews 4:11

48. Go in love -

Mark 12:28-34a; 1 Corinthians 16:14; Hebrews 13:1;

49. and never give in.

Romans 12:21; Gal. 6:9; I Corin. 9:24-27; Heb 12:1-17, 28, 29;

WHY ARE WE DOING THIS?

Well, that question may best be answered by walking through with us the questions we asked that got us here.

Starting with this one:

Is this all there is? Is this the BEST we can do?

How many times have we sat in church and wondered what was missing? How many times have we left, had lunch and can't remember ANYTHING from the sermon but the jokes? All the bickering and fighting and divisions and politics and money saps the joy and life out of us. Or worse, the life-crushing, dictatorial environment imposed by forced tithing and messages on complete subservience to the pastor and the leaders without whom you can't survive in the "world."

Can this really be what Jesus intended?

He wanted us to forgive seventy times seven and turn the other cheek and not let the sun go down on a dispute between brothers and He wanted us to be One Body. So if we stomp off mad after a business meeting doesn't go our way and start another church across the street - whose idea was that? Can't have been Jesus' idea. Must have been the other guy. There's only two choices, you know.

If we're listening to God and doing the will of Jesus - then how did we get to 33,000+ denominations, massive waste, billions in fraud per year, 50% of pastors addicted to porn, practically no demographic or attitudinal differences between us and the general population, millions migrating away, the youth nearly completely lost to culture, etc.?

Only one available conclusion, we're not following God's plan. Either God is in charge and he's completely incompetent - OR - we're not listening to God. If you look at the outcomes, it's clear we're losing this war. It must be that God isn't really in charge. If it's of Man it will fail, but if it's of God nothing can stand against it. And since we're failing, it must be that this was built largely under our own power.

If God isn't in charge, then whose idea must it have been to make it like this? Who benefits most?

Well, answering that one was really easy. If this is war and our churches are losing, then the enemy is benefiting most. If he was able to influence us in this direction, then he's done a really good job of co-opting or neutralizing all of our assets. We need to repent for being so blind and stupid.

What happened to miracles, healing, casting out demons, raising the dead, speaking in other languages and stuff like that? We're just not seeing them in America on any kind of a scale that you could call effective warfare. There are little flashes and anecdotal stories, but nothing that is completely consuming the press reports. Even in our own churches most of our denominations have decided this stuff isn't for today or

71

stopped when the Bible was completed. Where does it say that? How come these are happening all over the world but here? Is America God different than China God? Must be something else in the way, because He doesn't change. The two greatest weapons of revival are miracles and martyrdom. They are both evidence of a FEAR of the Lord and a belief that He is able to do anything. Seems like that's what we're missing.

So why did we give up our best weapons? Why do we mock the gifts of the Spirit?

If this is war, then the enemy will want to try to neutralize our best weapons and fix it so nobody trusts them or even wants them (or everybody is abusing them). We're such stupid sheep, we didn't even see it coming.

It's like if we were still in the Cold War with Russia and they decided to paint all their tanks pink and staff them with cute, fluffy girls in bikinis. They'd print calendars, it would be in the press all over the world, and every horny boy in America would have a picture of the Russian Tankgirls on his wall. Before you know it, we wouldn't be able to staff our own tanks because all the servicemen would be embarrassed to serve in tanks because "tanks are for girls". Then we start cutting back defense spending on tanks and then eliminate them altogether because we don't think the Russian Tankgirls are a threat and we can't staff our own tanks anyway because everybody is too embarrassed of the connotation against their manhood. Then Russia starts a land war, paints their tanks green again, puts beefy, hairy Russian guys in them - and we're in big trouble!

If there is a giant move of God and satan wants to neutralize it, all he has to do is have people like Benny Hinn endorse it and co-opt it. Then nobody will want to touch it! We're such stupid sheep. We gave up all our best weapons! Well, I want them back!! I'm sick of pop guns, I want a Cruise Missile and some Bunker Busters!!

And what happened to caring for the poor, hungry, sick and in prison? Aren't these on the final exam? (Matt. 25 - Remember the sheep and the goats?!)

If the enemy is in charge, these are the VERY LAST things he wants us doing - because it's the MOST like Jesus and ignoring them keeps us trapped in goathood. Since these ARE the very last thing we're currently doing, it must be additional confirmation that the enemy has been pulling the strings or at least got us so far off track that we're not even doing the CORE things Jesus wanted!

So, how much of the available income to our church structures is being diverted toward the poor and hungry and lonely and in prison? Probably less than 3%. Hard to say exactly, but it's tiny. That can't be good, you know, what with a final judgement coming where we're going to have to answer for all this stuff. Maybe we could change direction? Please?!

What happened to hearing the voice of God? What happened to being led by Him only?

Most churches will try to have you medicated or committed if you have the guts to say that God actually talks to you (unless you're the pastor). You see, we've built a system where one guy stands up front and tells everybody else what God wants them to do. We aren't actually teaching people how to hear God. They're talking about "priesthood of the believer" but they're always sticking a "priest" in the way to tell us what God wants. We're certainly not preaching pure obedience and repentance - which is the best, surest way to make sure you're hearing God. And we're not preaching that ANYONE can hear God, just those who have an "anointing" - or a diploma. And if you have a best-selling book and a big church, that's proof that must be hearing God REALLY well. We're such stupid sheep.

So are we just proposing ANOTHER "non-denominational" church?

NO! That's not it at all. What we're proposing is PRE-Denominational. Back the way it was in the beginning. The only Biblical model we have is the City Church. There was never to be any division in the Body. Saying you're Non-Denominational is still stepping aside from everyone else and dividing off into factions - whether you intend to or not. We just want to acknowledge that we ARE one body and sooner or later we're just going to HAVE to find a way to make this work. I highly doubt that any pastors in New Orleans were arguing about secondary doctrinal issues right after the hurricane - at least I certainly hope they're not. Is it going to take a world-wide disaster everywhere to get us to knock it off? Must be so, because that's what the book of Revelation predicts. The Christians will all be asleep and it will take seeing 2/3 of the world die to wake them up again.

So what do we do to turn this around?

You see, there are only two models of "church" in the Bible - the universal Body of Christ (the Bride) and the local city church (Jerusalem, Corinth, Ephesus, etc.). There were to be NO subdivisions of the city churches. That doesn't mean they all met in one building, that means they were united in one spirit. (So much so that the messages in Revelations 2-3 had application to a whole town, not just pieces of it.) The Greek word that got translated as "church" is "ekklesia" and simply means "those who are called out." There has always been a certain number of "those who were called out" in every town - but we just refuse to talk to each other because we disagree on Calvinism or the Rapture or whether to clap or sing fast music or which translation of the Bible to use or some other nonsense. Since it's all going to burn in the fire anyway, maybe we could just drop it. Whadaya say?

How exactly we're going to turn it around took a lot of praying and seeking God - and lots of repenting and obedience. It may require visual aids to fully explain. You see, in order for God to pour out His blessing and manifest glory, the vessel has to be in proper divine order and under His headship. It has to be operating according to His design and not it's own plans and intentions. And there is a progression that has to be observed. You can't take shortcuts. Of course, the enemy knows this, so he's tried to derail all of the steps along the progression so that we couldn't make any progress. And, he was very efficient and effective. We cannot proceed on the path we are on and expect God's blessing because we're NOT on God's path. That is, we're built on the wrong foundation, so anything we build will crumble. And by all accounts, everything we HAVE already built is crumbling around us. (See the Scary Stats section for more if you need proof of exactly how whacked everything is.)

There is a required progression and it goes like this:

Me   Home   City   Country   World

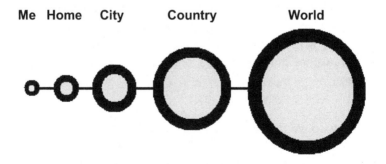

First, I get my own heart in order and under His headship. That means repentance, commitment to Him as Commander, walking in holiness and seeking Him only. Then I fix my marriage by getting it functioning according to His design and in obedience, then my home. Then all of the people that have accomplished THOSE start working on the Body of Christ in their town and get them acting as one body and in obedience. Then when the towns (the Body of Christ, not the real estate) get some critical mass, they start taking their state (or province), then their country, then the world. You CANNOT skip a step!!

So, why isn't this happening? There are certainly people who have their own lives and homes in order and under His headship. The enemy has been pounding away trying to divide families and enslave the people to sins of all kinds and has been very effective - but there are still those who haven't bowed their knee to the gods of the world. But, as near as we can tell (as of August of 2005) there were NO towns in America that were in divine order (fully under HIS headship only). There is a Body of Christ in every town, but they are divided up in little pieces all over and a divided house cannot stand. The strongholds and principalities of darkness that have responsibility for each town cannot be opposed by a divided Body of Christ. Since none of the Local Bodies (city churches) are in divine order, the strongholds can't be pulled down. We give them legal ground when we corporately continually violate Galatians 5:19-21. Since the towns are out of order, you can hardly expect that the states and countries could be right either.

So how do we restore the City Church in our town?

First you identify as many as possible of those who are in divine order and completely sold out to Christ (called out of the world). And you don't spend a single SECOND arguing about theology or style or practices and policies and rules of Man. That's what got us into this mess! You just find them and love on them as we're directed in I John and Romans 12 (and elsewhere). It could be a handful or it could be a thousand - it doesn't matter. If one can take on a thousand and two can take on ten thousand, then a representative handful is plenty to get started - as long as they are united and under proper headship (Jesus only!) and submitting to the giftings in each other AND the Lord is their Rock. (Deut. 32:30, Romans 12) (Please note that it's highly unlikely that you're going to accurately identify those people without having a very clear connection to the voice of God. You better get as much Holy Spirit in you as your cup can hold!)

Then you assert your rights as the Body and repent on behalf of the Body of Christ in your town and you hit your faces and wait on the Lord for the next step. In Romans 12, we offer our bodies as living sacrifices, holy and acceptable. It's the same here. You repent on behalf of the Body (should be plenty to repent for) and ask for its restoration and strengthening -- even to the very expense of your own souls (See Exodus 32:31-32, Romans 9:2-4, and the very nature of Jesus) and then you wait on the Lord for direction. You offer it as a living sacrifice - that means that you put it up on the altar and wait. YOU are the sacrifice. The sacrifice doesn't get to decide anything. It just lays there and waits. When God is ready, what He will do with the sacrifice is force it to stop conforming to the world, THEN it will be transformed by the renewing of it's mind and THEN it will know what is the perfect pleasing will of God and it can get to work.

This is NOT about building another new church building - God forbid! Or even having any structure that is recognizable to Man. It's just asserting the FACT that there IS a Body in your town (whether large or small) and that it needs to unite; set it's face like flint; get fully armored up against the enemy - and STAND. Then you can pray that blind eyes will see and deaf ears will hear and you can BE Jesus to the rest of the town. See Isaiah 58 - if you free the captives, break the chain, lift the yokes, feed the hungry, clothe the naked, STOP the malicious talk and pointing finger THEN He WILL turn and answer you and a bunch of good stuff happens - including rebuilding the walls on the ancient foundations (which is JESUS, not Man).

But as long as the Bodies are divided up all over town, the enemy has won. Read Judges 6. We cannot go to war against the rest of the world and expect God's blessing while there is still an altar of Baal in our own backyard. First you convert the altar back to the proper worship of God and THEN you go take on the big battle. And Gideon didn't have to fix every single altar to Baal in Israel, just the one in his own house.

How do we find the other "Living Stones" in our town?

What we need are those who are so full of Jesus they don't really fit in anywhere. At the rate we're losing leaders from the "institutional church" system (1 million+ a year in the USA), I suspect many of those are already out in the "wilderness" or have been told by God to stay in the church system even though they don't want to. Either way, when you do something radical that is purely and completely about Jesus, all the other radicals will smell it and come running. God will need to direct you on how to do that, but where we have developed tools that work, we'll communicate those along. More on that as it develops. (Please Note: We are NOT recommending you go try to get all the pastors in town to start talking to each other! If God tells you to do that, fine, but it seems like that's the path to ecumenical footsies, not to radical transformation and renewal. Besides, there may be whole churches where not a single solitary person - including the pastor - is truly a part of the

Body of Christ. Find them wherever they are, don't fall into the trap of assuming that the Body of Christ is the conglomeration of all the churches in town. It's just NOT.)

The main thing is that we have a lot to make up for, so if we start identifying those with the needs that are on the final exam (hungry, poor, naked, lonely, etc.) and we start meeting those needs in a big way (especially for Brethren), it will attract attention. But you have to be willing to proceed, even if no one else helps. Jesus went to the cross by himself. If you want to be like Jesus, you have to be willing to walk it alone.

We've made up some t-shirt designs that are so different than the norm, folks will have to pay attention. And nobody will wear them unless they are serious. For example, our "Need Prayer? Just Ask." shirt requires that you be willing to stop whatever you're doing, wherever you are and pray for someone AND know the right thing to pray. Are you really willing to completely snarl up a Walmart if God wants to start healing people? Are you willing to be late for work so a stranger can cry on your shoulder? People may not want to go to church and tithe, but nearly everyone will take some prayer. See the shirts here - www.cafepress.com/fotmartyrs . (We don't make hardly anything on these. They are printed on demand with no setup or screen charges! So the designs can be personalized to fit your town.) There are also books, music, art, and more there from people who are contributing their talents to help fund the work of the Kingdom. We've also been directed to work on resource exchanges to redirect the excess goods of those with too much to get them to those who have needs. And who knows what else is coming? God is very creative. The Church of Liberty has also been given a vision by God to build a massive computer network that will allow the Body of Christ in every town everywhere to link up in amazing ways and coordinate resources.

So what could happen if we take our towns?

Well, if we're right, then this is absolutely mandatory if God is going to pour out His blessing. We CANNOT proceed with the Nicolaitan ("nico"- in place of, "laitan" - laity) system we have and expect to see God's glory. We have to stop eating from the Tree of the Knowledge of Good and Evil - of laws and interpretations and rules and structures of Man - and start eating from the Tree of Life that Jesus offered once for all by His sacrifice. We have to free the captives. Free them from the world and sin and evil - and free them from the structures and systems and programs of "Churchianity". The proper way to do that is to point people toward Jesus with a real and firm expectation that He WILL talk to them and tell them individually and collectively what to do next. But we need to make sure we keep OURSELVES out of their way. We have to repent and we have to do it loud and strong. Read Ezekiel 9. ONLY those who are mourning and weeping and groaning because of the state of things are exempt from the death angel.

If we create new wineskins that are pure and have no trace of leaven in them, then God WILL pour out his New Wine.

Of course, none of us know how to do that, so HE is going to have to show us how and we're going to have to follow directions. He desperately wants to renew and restore His Church, but will not pour His full strength and power into our broken down old wineskins. What we need is transformation and that only comes when we stop conforming to the world - and like it or not, right now the institutional church system is sold out to the world. After transformation and renewal we can walk in His presence and know His will on all things and we can OBEY. Then I think we'll start to see Him express Himself in some big, attention-getting ways like the miracles other countries are seeing. When we take the towns, then we begin to free the captives and the workers (and the assets) begin to show up for the final harvest.

Oh yeah! And you can expect persecution to immediately begin once you commit to this path. So you better be willing and know what you're getting into. Better yet, be wishful and hopeful that persecution will come! If it comes because we are being more like Jesus (which is what He said would happen) then, serious persecution in the West is long overdue!!

Get it? Ready to restore your town for Jesus and put it back the way it was supposed to be all along? Even if you have to do it alone? We want to know who and where you are.

Although we're just getting started ourselves and have no staff and no budget - if you need it, we can provide websites, email, t-shirts designs, discussion boards, etc. until you get on your feet.

Even if you're not ready to take on your town yet, but you're willing to help us, we could sure use you. This is going to get completely crazy and it's going to go REALLY fast!

Just in case you didn't get all that, on Pentecost Sunday (2005) God released us to publish this website (www.TheChurchOfLiberty.com) to the internet and begin getting the word out.

If we're still being too subtle for you, try this:

We're blowing the trumpet and telling you to "Come out of her!!"

The New Song starts NOW! Praise God!! It's right on time.

Quick Thought:

In the age of computers and The Hair Club for Men, maybe you're not impressed anymore by a God who knows every hair on your head.

How about this?

Every atom in the universe has a
unique personal name and God named it.

Not a serial number – a NAME – quark "Susie," proton "Fred," molecule "Erma," muon "Jeff."

Every leaf, every snowflake, every grain of sand, every solar flare, every radio wave.

He knows how and where it started, how and where it will end and everything it will bump into in between. And He knew it all before He made the Universe.

Is THAT big enough for you?!

Because **THAT** is the size of the God we made angry with our stupid, petty selfishness.

We might want to say we're sorry. Like RIGHT NOW.

WAS JESUS A LIBERAL?

Well the short answer is, "No." But He wasn't really a Conservative either. Labels don't really fit Jesus very well.

Consider this:

Jesus sounds sort of Liberal

- Jesus cared about workers' rights.

- Jesus was into recycling and not wasting resources.

- Jesus criticized the legalistic Pharisees (conservatives) very strongly.

- Jesus had disciples that were anti-authority, anti-big government Zealots.

- Jesus hung out with the people rejected by society.

- Jesus cared for the handicapped and hurting.

- Jesus cared about little children and cursed anyone that would hurt them.

- Jesus cared about the earth and it's health.

- Jesus promised the destruction of the Temple, the sign of God's favor on a specific people.

- Jesus was multi-cultural and embraced diversity by reaching out to those different or dirty.

- Jesus criticized the "Rich" for their selfishness and lack of care for the poor.

- Jesus urged that all share resources as there was a need.

- Jesus had "blue collar" disciples.

- Jesus went out and talked to the masses.

- Jesus supported and strengthened the role of women in a highly patriarchal culture.

- Jesus said He was a servant to all and washed the feet of His disciples.

Jesus sounds sort of Conservative

- Jesus cared about the rights of the land-owner and business man.

- Jesus talked about money a lot and not always critically.

- Jesus said He came to fulfill the Law, not to break it.

- Jesus criticized the Sadducees (liberals) for their esoteric arguments instead of action.

- Jesus hung out with Pharisees (conservatives) frequently - even had them among His disciples.

- Jesus hung out with rich people. Even government officials.

- Jesus cared about stability in government and said to pray for them, not fight against them.

- Jesus never urged anyone to take the country by force.

- Jesus cursed a fig tree when it didn't bear fruit and then it shriveled up and died.

- Jesus promised the rebuilding of an eternal, all-encompassing Temple over which He would be King.

- Jesus was focused first on His group (the Jews) and only reluctantly reached out to others later.

- Jesus affirmed the right of the rich to enjoy what they have.

- Jesus had "white collar" disciples.

- Jesus met behind closed doors with influential leaders.

- Jesus asserted that the role of the men in bringing His plan was critical.

- Jesus said He was to be King and absolute ruler.

Jesus sounds like Jesus

- Jesus was willing to set aside all of His desires and die a brutal death to save all of us.

- Jesus loved everyone He came into contact with - even when He was yelling at them.

- Jesus prayed and cried over the destruction that was coming to Jerusalem and wished they would listen.

- Jesus picked disciples from the most unlikely places, completely outside of either camp.

- Jesus was willing to see earth pass away so that it could be renewed.

- Jesus prayed forgiveness for his enemies, even when they were nailing Him to a cross.

- Jesus performed miracles and then told people to keep their mouth shut about it.

- Jesus walked right into the synagogues and quoted their own words against them.

- Jesus said He was the Son of God. In fact, He said He was "I AM" - which is the name of God (from Sinai).

- Jesus sacrificed His life to wash away our sins.

You can't put a man-made label on Jesus that easily. He was unique. Never in human history has one person had so much impact - no matter how much financial, political, or military resources were behind them - and all of this in just three years. Jesus had none of those assets. Just His words and the testimony of His life.

Believe what you want about Jesus, but there are only two choices:

- EITHER -- He was a raving lunatic and ego-maniac

- OR -- He was the Son of God and spoke Truth every time He opened His mouth.

Believing He was a wise man or a prophet or just a smart guy is NOT an option.

He said over and over that He WAS God, that He was the Son of God, that He was to die and be resurrected, that He was the only option for the redemption of sin, that He was eternal, that He was going to destroy the Temple in three days - and much more.

So which is it? Nearly all of His disciples died as martyrs. Nearly all died horrible, painful deaths (crucified, quartered, boiled in oil, crucified upside down, eaten by lions, hacked to death, stoned, whipped, etc.). If this was all made up, then why didn't any of them renounce it? Would you die for a man you knew to be a fraud?

Hmmmm.

Musical Interlude -
Feel free to sing along

Jesus loves the little children,
all the children of the world

Red and yellow, black and white,
they are precious in His sight.

Jesus loves the little children of the world.

Very nice. Not real complicated, is it?

So why are we spending the vast majority of all the Christian money on the comforts and indulgences of the white ones?

Who would like to go explain that to the red, yellow and black ones?

Quick Thought:

What if in the back of the Wall Street Journal there were the Stock pages, the Mutual Fund pages AND a list of all the Christian ministries and how much treasure in heaven they were earning per dollar spent?

A complete listing of the "exchange rate" the ROI for each ministry. Hmmmm...

Would you dump the stock you're holding and invest somewhere else?

RIGHT INSTINCT, WRONG CURRENCY

(Matt. 6; I Pet. 1; Rev. 3:17-21; Rev. 18; I Cor. 3; Matt. 23:17;
Eph. 2:6-8; Col. 1:27; Matt. 24:9-14; Matt. 25)

I Peter 1:18-19 - *"For you know that it was not with perishable things such as silver or gold that you were redeemed from the empty way of life handed down to you from your forefathers, but with the precious blood of Christ, a lamb without blemish or defect."*

Matthew 6:19-24 - *"Do not store up for yourselves treasures on earth, where moth and rust destroy, and where thieves break in and steal. But store up for yourselves treasures in heaven, where moth and rust do not destroy, and where thieves do not break in and steal. For where your treasure is, there your heart will be also. The eye is the lamp of the body. If your eyes are good, your whole body will be full of light. But if your eyes are bad, your whole body will be full of darkness. If then the light within you is darkness, how great is that darkness! "No one can serve two masters. Either he will hate the one and love the other, or he will be devoted to the one* *and despise the other. You cannot serve both God and Money."*

Matthew 6:31-34 - *"So do not worry, saying, 'What shall we eat?' or 'What shall we drink?' or 'What shall we wear?' For the pagans run after all these things, and your heavenly Father knows that you need them. But seek first his kingdom and his righteousness, and all these things will be given to you as well. Therefore do not worry about tomorrow, for tomorrow will worry about itself. Each day has enough trouble of its own."*

What a blessing it is to be an American! If your hope is for a comfortable life, health, opportunities to accumulate assets - what a blessing. If your hope is for spiritual purity and being like Christ - what a curse it is to live here! The "American Dream" trumpeted around the world that urges the poor, downtrodden, huddled masses to come to us is the vision that they could work hard, make a million dollars, get a big car, a big house and a pretty blonde wife in a bikini. If not them, then maybe their kids.

Do you see that God has blessed this nation from the very beginning with relative peace, with an entrepreneurial spirit, with a great work ethic, with capital and energy enough to accomplish nearly any task? The problem is our continuous misunderstanding of the nature of the economy of the universe. Without a great revival movement every fifty years in this country (since 1750), there might be no signs of Christian love left. We would have long since been absorbed by the consumer mentality. Even now we are in grave danger as the church unrepentantly becomes more and more like the world.

We've been blessed by God with the right instincts - massive accumulation of treasure through hard work and entrepreneurial thinking. But we've ignored the specific instructions in the Bible about what money is FOR. We've arrogantly chosen the easy parts of the Bible and dismissed those that draw us into conflict with worldy culture. (We are not being persecuted **because** we are not trying to be like Christ. As soon as a big enough movement of Christians decides to throw off this culture and live as Christ commanded, persecution will start in America. Enough of them might even be seen as a threat to our economic safety and national security.)

The Bible says we're to store up treasure in Heaven where it won't rust and thieves can't steal. If we are to covet anything, it is this. The eternal treasure is the thing. Don't you get it? That's what dollars are for! If God has blessed you with more than your basic needs, every single extra dollar should be used to purchase Heavenly treasure. Any other use of them is selfishness, apostasy and ultimately, idolatry. Not my words - I'm not happy about it either. I stand condemned the same as anyone else. But you can't leave the verses cited above out of the Scriptures and still honestly say your desire is to be like Christ.

Imagine someone offered you Microsoft stock or Hewlett-Packard stock when those guys were still working in their garages. Better yet, imagine if you absolutely, positively knew what that stock would be worth someday. You knew it was a winner. Would you buy into them? Would you sacrifice some current luxury to help them grow - in exchange for the massive long-term payoff?

When God finally got through to me and helped me see this, all of my American business instincts kicked into overdrive. If every dollar is entrusted to me **SO THAT** I can use it to buy treasure in Heaven, then I want maximum return on investment for every single dollar. See? Makes perfect sense. So I went on a search to first see how my money was currently being used and then find who might be a better investment. As it turns out, the "stocks" I'd been buying through denominational structures and "Big Church" programs have a TERRIBLE yield in Heaven. I can't say they're all losers, but they were definitely under-performing their potential.

I want to find those mighty warriors, those servants of the Cross, those who are truly being obedient and living like Christ; those who when they pray you just know God hears them; those who have eternal fruit flying off of them like crazy; those who are caring for the poor and sick and lost; those who are storing up treasure in heaven faster than anybody else - then I want in on it. I want to buy a share in their pile of treasure. (Matt. 10:41-42) I want to support them, urge them on and get out of their way. I want a stake in that eternal reward. And if I have a hot tip that's going to make me a fortune, I want to tell my friends and my family and my employees and even strangers on the bus!

Our search for who is the hottest stock led us first to Gospel For Asia (www.GFA.org), although we are now finding others and will seek to highlight them at every opportunity. For example, the native missionaries that GFA supports are amazing warriors of the faith, going out to hostile regions on a one way ticket with grim determination to win souls for Christ or die trying. They sleep on stone floors, live on one or two dollars a day, pray for hours, preach fearlessly and raise up mighty churches of fearless disciples - and when God thinks it will help, mighty miracles make their way easier. All for a total ministry cost of $1000 to $1500 per year in most cases.

Western missionaries sent through our denominational structures often cost $100,000 per year. Average investment in one missionary family can exceed $500,000 with an average time on the field of just three years. Many prepare and never go at all. Private schools or tutors for their kids, healthcare, retirement funds, furloughs, maids, chauffeurs, security guards, language training, internet access and more - may all be required costs for these. Not to mention the lost potential in ministry momentum of having to come back to fund-raise periodically. (I don't question the motives of the missionaries. I speak from experience here, having grown up in that life.) Even with all of this, foreign missions is less than 5% of total church spending. The rest we spend on our local programs, buildings and staffs.

Our website is just an expression of that yearning for stewardship and has become a place to educate about the HORRIBLE job we're doing in the American church of spending our dollars wisely to get maximum yield in Heaven. I urge you, test yourself, your company, your church, your denomination, your charities. What is their true yield in Heavenly treasure? Seek maximum profit in the eternal currency.

I want my family, my employees, you and your family and a thousand thousand other Brothers and Sisters to be in a giant receiving line where we get to kiss and hug the souls brought into heaven by the labor of those on the field that we supported from the blessings of our wealth. If Heaven is forever, I want that line to stretch farther than I can see. I want that line to last for YEARS.

The "Prosperity Gospel" ministries are right, they're living in their reward. This is it. Enjoy it while you can. What are those HUNDREDS OF MILLIONS of dollars per year their ministries are bringing in going to buy them in Heaven? What kind of accountability are we getting? How much is going to ministry and not their own pockets? What treasure in Heaven is being accumulated? Really needed that private jet and multi-million dollar house did they? Let's see what Jesus has to say about it when we all come to account. I pray urgently for them to have the heart of Zacchaeus before it's too late. Repent and make restitution.

As for me and my house, we'll invest in those who are living like Christ. GFA sends 100% of missions donations to evangelism on the field to the most unreached. Even the receptionist and the shipping guy have to volunteer or else raise their own salaries from personal supporters. MILLIONS of souls a year are being reached. Ten new churches planted every day.

Which one do YOU want a piece of?

Research the ministries. Be smart. Invest wisely. Demand accountability and efficiency. Visit www.ECFA.org and www.MinistryWatch.org. If they can't be trusted with the little things, they can't be trusted with the big things. Would Jesus of Nazareth drive a Bentley or a Rolls Royce? Have gold faucets in His bathroom? There are some serious wolves out there amongst the sheep.

Whether entrusted with a little or a lot, we'll all be called to account for our stewardship of God's blessings.

ARE YOU KIDDING ME?!
SCARY STATS AND FACTS

This is a compilation of the scariest, most embarrassing, most shocking statistics and information about the Church and it's affairs. We don't quote anything haphazardly without having good documentation and sources. If you have stats that you think we need to hear, find the source material and email us.

(Mostly from World Christian Trends, William Carey Library, David Barrett & Todd Johnson, 2001. The summary and analysis of the annual Christian mega-census.) Available for purchase online or from our site.

Assets of the Church

- US Christians control TRILLIONS in assets while at any given time 200,000,000 Christians starve.

- 78 countries each have Great Commission (evangelical) Christians whose cumulative personal incomes exceed US$1 billion a year. (WCT, page 3, Table 1-1)

Financial Fraud in the Church

- Annual church embezzlements by top custodians exceed the entire cost of all foreign missions worldwide. Emboldened by lax procedures, trusted church treasurers are embezzling from the Church $5,500,000 PER DAY. That's $16,000,000,000 per YEAR! That's Billion - with a "B"! (WCT, page 3, Table 1-1) {For reference: TOTAL Christian spending on foreign missions - $15 Billion. God forgive us!} (WCT, page 8, Table 1-4)

- Criminal penalties against clergy in sexual abuse cases now exceed $1 billion, causing a number of churches, dioceses, and even denominations to be forced into bankruptcy. (WCT, page 3, Table 1-1)

- Each year 600,000 full-time ordained workers (clergy,ministers,missionaries) reach retiring age; 150,000 then discover that their employers provide no old-age pensions. (WCT, page 3, Table 1-1)

Wasteful Spending by the Church

- Most Christian bodies insist on full accountability to the last cent in finance {But not very well. See above.}, but ignore or even decry statistics about Christian workers and ministries. (WCT, page 3)

- Less than 1% of Christian revenue is spent on evangelism to the most unreached. (WCT, page 81)

- 40% of the church's entire global foreign mission resources are being deployed to just 10 over-saturated countries already possessing strong citizen-run home ministries. (WCT, p. 3, Table 1-1)

- All costs of ministry divided by number of baptisms per year. Cost per baptism in India - $9803 per person. Cost per baptism in the United States - $1,550,000 per person. (WCT, page 520-529)

- Every year the churches hold a megacensus costing $1.1 billion, sending out 10 million questionnaires in 3,000 languages, which covers 180 major religious subjects. (WCT, page 3, Table 1-1)

- Christians spend more on the annual audits of their churches and agencies ($810 million) than on all their workers in the non-Christian world. (WCT, page 3, Table 1-1)

- The total cost of Christian outreach averages $330,000 for each and every newly baptized person. (USA $1,551,000, India $9,800, Mozambique $1,400, etc.) (WCT, page 3, Table 1-1 and pages 520 - 529)

- Non-Christian countries have been found to have 227 million Bibles in place in their midst, more than needed to serve all Christians, but poorly distributed. (WCT, page 3, Table 1-1)

- 91% of all Christian outreach/evangelism does not target non-Christians but targets other Christians in World C {>95 Evangelized, >60% Christian} countries, cities, peoples, populations, or situations. (WCT, page 81)

- Each year,180 million Bibles and New Testaments are wasted - lost, destroyed, or disintegrated - due to incompetence, hostility, bad planning, or inadequate manufacture. (WCT, page 3, Table 1-1)

- Books primarily about Jesus in today's libraries number 175,000 different titles in 500 languages, increasing by 4 newly published every day. As in all scientific research, 70% of all new Christian books and published articles will never be quoted in print by their peers, ever. (WCT, page 3, Table 1-1)

Persecution of the Church

- More than 70% of all Christians now live in countries where they are experiencing persecution. In some cases EXTREME persecution. (WCT, page 32)

- 14 million converted Hindus, Buddhists, and Muslims have opted to remain within those religions in order to witness for Christ as active believers in Jesus as Lord. (WCT, page 3, Table 1-1)

Growth of the Church

- From 3 million in AD 1500, evangelicals have grown to 648 million worldwide, 54% being Non-Whites. (WCT, page 3)

- The country with the fastest Christian expansion ever is China, now at 10,000 new converts every day. (WCT, page 3)

Missions and the Church

- Some 250 of the 300 largest international Christian organizations regularly mislead the Christian public by publishing demonstrably incorrect or falsified progress statistics. (WCT, page 3, Table 1-1)

- Christian triumphalism - not as pride in huge numbers, but as publicized self-congratulation - is rampant in most churches, agencies, and ministries. (WCT, page 3, Table 1-1)

- All costs of ministry divided by number of baptisms per year. Cost per baptism in India - $9803 per person. Cost per baptism in the United States - $1,550,000 per person. (WCT, pages 520-529)

- It costs Christians 700 times more money to baptize converts in rich World C countries (Switzerland) than in poor World A countries (Nepal). (WCT, pages 520-529)

- Percent of Christian resources in countries that are already more than 60% Christian - 91%. Percent spent in countries where less than half the people have EVER heard of Jesus - 0.03%. (WCT, page 81)

- It is estimated that Christians worldwide spend around $8 BILLION dollars PER YEAR going to the more than 500 conferences to TALK about missions. That's more than HALF the total spent DOING missions.

- Everywhere on Earth can now be targeted with at least 3 of the 45 varieties of effective evangelism. (WCT, page 3)

- 818 unevangelized ethnolinguistic peoples have never been targeted by any Christian agencies ever. (WCT, page 3)

- Over 20 centuries Christians have announced 1,500 global plans to evangelize the world; most failed; 250 plans focused on AD 2000 fell massively short of stated goals. (WCT, page 3, Table 1-1)

- Mainland China's Christians have thousands of trained workers poised to begin evangelizing the world de novo (all over again) soon after AD 2000. (WCT, page 3, Table 1-1)

- Regular listeners to Christian programs over secular or religious radio/TV stations rose from 22% of the world in 1980 to 30% in 2000. (WCT, page 3, Table 1-1)

- Out of 648 million Great Commission Christians, 70% have never been told about the world's 1.6 billion unevangelized individuals. (WCT, page 3, Table 1-1)

- The 3 least cost-effective countries over 1 million in population for Christian outreach are: Japan, Switzerland, Denmark. (WCT, page 3, Table 1-1 and pages 520-529)

- The 3 most cost-effective countries over 1 million in population for Christian outreach are: Mozambique, Ethiopia, Tanzania. (WCT, page 3, Table 1-1 and pages 520-529)

- Per hour of ministry, the 5 megapeoples most responsive to Christianity, Christ, and the gospel are: Khandeshi, Awadhi, Magadhi, Bai, Berar Marathi. (WCT, page 3, Table 1-1)

- Per hour of ministry, the 5 megapeoples least responsive to Christianity, Christ, and the gospel are: Swedish, Russian, Lithuanian, Polish, Georgian . (WCT, page 3, Table 1-1)

Denominations of the Church

- Currently there are over 33,000 Christian denominations in the United States. (37,000+ as of 2005!) (WCT, page 33)

- A huge new Christian nonconfessional megabloc, the Independents/Postdenominationalists, is growing rapidly and numbers 19% of all Christians. These 386 million Independents in 220 countries have no interest in and no use for historic denominationalist Christianity. (WCT, p.3, Table 1-1)

- From only one million in AD 1900, Pentecostals/ Charismatics/ Neocharismatics have mushroomed to 524 million affiliated (with unaffiliated believers, 602 million). (WCT, page 3, Table 1-1)

Martyrdom

- Over the last 20 centuries, and in all 238 countries, more than 70 million Christians have been martyred – killed, executed, murdered - for Christ. (WCT, page 3 and page 32)

- More Christians have been martyred in the last 100 years than all years since AD 30 combined. (WCT page 32)

Global Population Issues

- Despite BILLIONS of dollars spent by dozens of denominations toward over a hundred major programs to fulfill the Great Commission by the year 2000, we didn't even keep up with population growth, much less reach the 2 billion unreached. (WCT, page 3) Evidently no apologies are forthcoming for the giant waste of assets and broken promises.

- 124 million new souls begin life on Earth each year, but Christianity's 4,000 foreign mission agencies baptize only 4 million new persons a year. (WCT, page 3, Table 1-1)

- Since AD 1900,Christian urbanites have exploded from 100 million in 500 cities to 1,160 million in 5,000 cities. (WCT, page 3, Table 1-1)

Unreached Peoples

- Out of 648 million Great Commission Christians, 70% have never been told about world's 1.6 billion unevangelized individuals. (WCT, page 3, Table 1-1)

- There are thousands of language groups who do not have a SINGLE page of the Bible in their language.

- 98.7% of people have access to scripture in 6,700 languages leaving 78 million in 6,800 languages with no access at all. (WCT, page 44)

- The majority of the unreached people groups are in countries that are restricted access. Western missionaries may not even be able to get to them. (WCT, page 3, Table 1-1)

- Despite Christ's command to evangelize, 67% of all humans from AD 30 to the present day have never even heard of his name. (WCT, page 3, Table 1-1)

- 648 million Christians today (called Great Commission Christians) are active in Christ's world mission; 1,352 million Christians ignore this mission. (WCT, page 3, Table 1-1)

- Organized Christianity has total contact with 3,590 religions but no contact at all with 353 other religions and their over 500 million adherents. (WCT, page 3, Table 1-1)

Micro-Lending Stats

- We can help a Brother or Sister start a business in India with a loan of as little as $25.

Had Enough Yet? It gets worse! We're stuffing the Fattest and starving the Hungriest!

KEY:

World A are the 38 countries that are primarily unevangelized. <50% unreached (1.6 Billion souls). Mostly Asia and North Africa - often called the 10/40 Window.

World B are the 59 countries evangelized by not converted. >50% reached but <60% Christian (2.9 billion souls)

World C are the 141 countries primarily or predominantly Christian already. >95% Evangelized and >60% Christian (2 billion souls) These are mostly the "West" - North, Central and South America, Europe, Southern Africa, and Australia.

Broadcasting (radio/TV) per year - Total spend $5.8 Billion

World A - $6 Million (0.01%)
World B - $226M (3.9%)
World C - $5,568M (96.0%)

Foreign Missions Money per year – Total spend $15 Billion

World A - $250M (1.7%)
World B - $1,750M (11.7%)
World C - $13,000M (86.6%)

Finance (church/agency) per yr – Total spend $270 Billion

World A - $188M (0.01%)
World B - $1,370M (5.1%)
World C - $256 **Billion** (94.8%)

Scripture distribution per year – Total 4,600 million pieces

World A - 20 Million (0.4%)
World B - 680M (14.5%)
World C - 3,900M (84.8%)

(Plus 11 other scales that all look about the same. Tracts, Scripture languages, Literature, Periodicals, Computers, Full-time workers, Computer users, Foreign Missionaries, Home Missionaries, Lay leadership. WCT, page 55.)

Keep reading, there's more – and it's worse.

From Page 80 - "Where should foreign missionaries work?" **& Page 520 -** "A comparative listing of 6-instrument Great Commission Instrument Panels for the globe's 77 largest countries, each with over 10 million population."

Canada (total population 31,147,000)

Unevangelized - 2.2%

Evangelized but non-Christian - 18.3%

Christian (of one sort or another) - 79.5%

(self-described, includes Catholics)

Evangelization percent - 97.8%

Evangelistic offers per person per year - 331

Cost effectiveness (Cost per baptism) $1,189,000

USA (total population 278,357,00)

Unevangelized - 1.5%

Evangelized but non-Christian - 13.8%

Christian (of one sort or another) - 84.7%

Evangelization percent - 98.5%

Offers per person per year - 368

Cost effectiveness (Cost per baptism) $1,551,000

Australia (total population 18,880,000)

Unevangelized - 1.6%

Evangelized but non-Christian - 19.1%

Christian (of one sort or another) - 79.3%

Evangelization percent - 98%

Offers per person per year - 336

Cost effectiveness (Cost per baptism) $1,104,000

Japan (total population 126,714,000)

Unevangelized - 33.1%

Evangelized but non-Christian - 63.3%

Christian (of one sort or another) - 3.6%

Evangelization percent - 60%

Offers per person per year - 6

Cost effectiveness (Cost per baptism) $2,721,000

Germany (total population 82,220,000)

Unevangelized - 2.4%

Evangelized but non-Christian - 21.8%

Christian (of one sort or another) - 75.8%

Evangelization percent - 97%

Offers per person per year - 381

Cost effectiveness (Cost per baptism) $2,119,000

Mexico (total population 98,881,000)

Unevangelized - 0.2%

Evangelized but non-Christian - 3.5%

Christian (of one sort or another) - 96.3%

Evangelization percent - 99.8%

Offers per person per year - 560

Cost effectiveness (Cost per baptism) $147,100

But what about the "poor" countries? What kind of cost effectiveness per dollar do we see there?

India (total population 1,013,662,000)

Unevangelized - 40.7%

Evangelized but non-Christian - 53.1%

Christian (of one sort or another) - 6.2%

Evangelization percent - 59.3%

Offers per person per year - 13

Cost effectiveness (Cost per baptism) $9,800

China (total population 1,262,557,000)

Unevangelized - 35.2%

Evangelized but non-Christian - 57.7%

Christian (of one sort or another) - 7.1%

Evangelization percent - 64.8%

Offers per person per year - 16

Cost effectiveness (Cost per baptism) $15,800

Indonesia (total population 212,107,000)

Unevangelized - 37.2%

Evangelized but non-Christian - 49.7%

Christian (of one sort or another) - 13.1%

Evangelization percent - 62.8%

Offers per person per year - 29
Cost effectiveness (Cost per baptism) $40,800

Afghanistan (total population 22,720,000)

Unevangelized - 70.4%
Evangelized but non-Christian - 29.6%
Christian (of one sort or another) - 0.1%
Evangelization percent - 29.7%
Offers per person per year - < 1
Cost effectiveness (Cost per baptism) $30,400

Cambodia (total population 11,168,000)

Unevangelized - 50.9%
Evangelized but non-Christian - 48.0%
Christian (of one sort or another) - 1.1%
Evangelization percent - 49.1%
Offers per person per year - 1
Cost effectiveness (Cost per baptism) $4,300

Bangladesh (total population 129,155,000)

Unevangelized - 42.8%
Evangelized but non-Christian - 56.5%
Christian (of one sort or another) - 0.7%
Evangelization percent - 57.2%
Offers per person per year - 1
Cost effectiveness (Cost per baptism) $7,200

Most of the stats from "An AD 2001 reality check: 50 new facts and figures about trends and issues concerning empirical global Christianity today." (from Table 1-1 and elsewhere in World Christian Trends, William Carey Library, David Barrett & Todd Johnson.)

REALLY SCARY SCRIPTURES

Is your heart so hard that you can't see our own guilt? Does the Word of God stand against you?

Jeremiah 5:26-31 (all NIV) - 26 "Among my people are wicked men who lie in wait like men who snare birds and like those who set traps to catch men. 27 Like cages full of birds, their houses are full of deceit; they have become rich and powerful 28 and have grown fat and sleek. Their evil deeds have no limit; they do not plead the case of the fatherless to win it, they do not defend the rights of the poor. 29 Should I not punish them for this?" declares the LORD . "Should I not avenge myself on such a nation as this? **30 "A horrible and shocking thing has happened in the land: 31 The prophets prophesy lies, the priests rule by their own authority, and my people love it this way. But what will you do in the end?**

Jeremiah 6:16-17 - 16 This is what the LORD says: "Stand at the crossroads and look; ask for the ancient paths, **ask where the good way is, and walk in it, and you will find rest for**

your souls. But you said, 'We will not walk in it.' 17 I appointed watchmen over you and said, 'Listen to the sound of the trumpet!' But you said, 'We will not listen.'

Luke 6:24-26 - But woe to you who are rich, for you have already received your comfort. Woe to you who are well fed now, for you will go hungry. Woe to you who laugh now, for you will mourn and weep. Woe to you when all men speak well of you, for that is how their fathers treated the false prophets.

Matthew 19:21-24 - Jesus answered, "If you want to be perfect, go, sell your possessions and give to the poor, and you will have treasure in heaven. Then come, follow me." When the young man heard this, he went away sad, because he had great wealth. Then Jesus said to his disciples, "I tell you the truth, it is hard for a rich man to enter the kingdom of heaven. Again I tell you, it is easier for a camel to go through the eye of a needle than for a rich man to enter the kingdom of God."

I Timothy 6:21 - Command those who are rich in this present world not to be arrogant nor to put their hope in wealth, which is so uncertain, but to put their hope in God, who richly provides us with everything for our enjoyment. Command them to do good, to be rich in good deeds, and to be generous and willing to share. In this way they will lay up treasure for themselves as a firm foundation for the coming age, so that they may take hold of the life that is truly life.

I Timothy 4:1-2, 6 - The Spirit clearly says that in later times some will abandon the faith and follow deceiving spirits and things taught by demons. Such teachings come through hypocritical liars, whose consciences have been seared as with a hot iron. If you point these things out to the brothers, you will be a good minister of Christ Jesus, brought up in the truths of the faith and of the good teaching that you have followed.

II Timothy 3:1-5 - But mark this: There will be terrible times in the last days. People will be lovers of themselves, lovers of money, boastful, proud, abusive, disobedient to their parents, ungrateful, unholy, without love, unforgiving, slanderous, without self-control, brutal, not lovers of the good, treacherous, rash, conceited, lovers of pleasure rather than lovers of God --- having a form of godliness, but denying its power. Have nothing to do with them.

Luke 12:15-21 - Then he said to them, "Watch out! Be on your guard against all kinds of greed; a man's life does not consist in the abundance of his possessions." And he told them this parable: "The ground of a certain rich man produced a good crop. He thought to himself, 'What shall I do? I have no place to store my crops.' "Then he said, 'This is what I'll do. I will tear down my barns and build bigger ones, and there I will store all my grain and my goods. 19 And I'll say to myself, "You have plenty of good things laid up for many years. Take life easy; eat, drink and be merry." ' "But God said to him, 'You fool! This very night your life will be demanded from you. Then who will get what you have prepared for yourself?' "This is how it will be with anyone who stores up things for himself but is not rich toward God."

Micah 7 - 1 What misery is mine! I am like one who gathers summer fruit at the gleaning of the vineyard; there is no cluster of grapes to eat, none of the early figs that I crave. **2 The godly have been swept from the land; not one upright man remains. All men lie in wait to shed blood; each hunts his brother with a net. 3 Both hands are skilled in doing evil; the ruler demands gifts, the judge accepts bribes, the powerful dictate what they desire- they all conspire together. 4 The best of them is like a brier, the most**

upright worse than a thorn hedge. **The day of your watchmen has come, the day God visits you. Now is the time of their confusion. 5 Do not trust a neighbor; put no confidence in a friend. Even with her who lies in your embrace be careful of your words. 6 For a son dishonors his father, a daughter rises up against her mother, a daughter-in-law against her mother in-law - a man's enemies are the members of his own household. 7 But as for me, I watch in hope for the LORD , I wait for God my Savior; my God will hear me.** 8 Do not gloat over me, my enemy! Though I have fallen, I will rise. Though I sit in darkness, the LORD will be my light. **9 Because I have sinned against him, I will bear the LORD's wrath, until he pleads my case and establishes my right. He will bring me out into the light; I will see his righteousness.** 10 Then my enemy will see it and will be covered with shame, she who said to me, "Where is the LORD your God?" My eyes will see her downfall; even now she will be trampled underfoot like mire in the streets. 11 The day for building your walls will come, the day for extending your boundaries. 12 In that day people will come to you from Assyria and the cities of Egypt, even from Egypt to the Euphrates and from sea to sea and from mountain to mountain. 13 The earth will become desolate because of its inhabitants, as the result of their deeds. 14 Shepherd your people with your staff, the flock of your inheritance, which lives by itself in a forest, in fertile pasturelands. Let them feed in Bashan and Gilead as in days long ago. **15 "As in the days when you came out of Egypt, I will show them my wonders." 16 Nations will see and be ashamed, deprived of all their power. They will lay their hands on their mouths and their ears will become deaf. 17 They will lick dust like a snake, like creatures that crawl on the ground. They will come trembling out of their dens; they will turn in fear to the LORD our God and will be afraid** of you. **18 Who is a God like you, who pardons sin and forgives the transgression of the remnant of his inheritance? You do not stay angry forever but delight to show mercy. 19 You will again have compassion on us; you will tread our sins underfoot and hurl all our iniquities into the depths of the sea. 20 You will be true to Jacob, and show mercy to Abraham, as you pledged on oath to our fathers in days long ago.**

Ezekiel 9 - 1 Then I heard him call out in a loud voice, "Bring the guards of the city here, each with a weapon in his hand." 2 And I saw six men coming from the direction of the upper gate, which faces north, each with a deadly weapon in his hand. With them was a man clothed in linen who had a writing kit at his side. They came in and stood beside the bronze altar. 3 Now the glory of the God of Israel went up from above the cherubim, where it had been, and moved to the threshold of the temple. Then the LORD called to the man clothed in linen who had the writing kit at his side 4 and saidto him, **"Go throughout the city of Jerusalem and put a mark on the foreheads of those who grieve and lament over all the detestable things that are done in it."** 5 As I listened, he said to the others, **"Follow him through the city and kill, without showing pity or compassion. 6 Slaughter old men, young men and maidens, women and children, but do not touch anyone who has the mark. Begin at my sanctuary."** So they began with the elders who were in front of the temple. 7 Then he said to them, "Defile the temple and fill the courts with the slain. Go!" So they went out and began killing throughout the city. 8 While they were killing and I was left alone, I fell facedown, crying out, "Ah, Sovereign LORD! Are you going to destroy the entire remnant of Israel in this outpouring of your wrath on Jerusalem?" 9 He answered me, **"The sin of the house of Israel and Judah is exceedingly great; the land is full of bloodshed and the city is full of injustice. They say,**

'The LORD has forsaken the land; the LORD does not see.' **10 So I will not look on them with pity or spare them, but I will bring down on their own heads what they have done."** 11 Then the man in linen with the writing kit at his side brought back word, saying, "I have done as you commanded."

Jeremiah 51:11-13 - 11 "Sharpen the arrows, take up the shields! The LORD has stirred up the kings of the Medes, because his purpose is to destroy Babylon. The LORD will take vengeance, vengeance for his temple. 12 Lift up a banner against the walls of Babylon! Reinforce the guard, station the watchmen, prepare an ambush! The LORD will carry out his purpose, his decree against the people of Babylon. 13 **You who live by many waters and are rich in treasures, your end has come, the time for you to be cut off.**

{Connect this with Revelations 18, the destruction of Babylon. Which many believe to mean America.}

There's lots more! Read Hosea. That'll scare you!! Or Ezekiel.

They're not just about the nation of Israel – they apply to America, to the Church, to your town, to YOU!

Anytime someone does Bad Behavior X, they should expect Punishment Y as a result.

Well, whatever Israel did to bring on God's judgement – the Church of America is doing X times 1000!!

We should expect God to react NOW the same as He did THEN.

WHAT EXACTLY IS THE "GREAT COMMISSION"?

This term is applied to the final command of Jesus just before He ascended into heaven following His resurrection. It is the command to not just go and evangelize, but to train and prepare and an assurance that when you do it HIS way, signs and wonders will follow.

Depending on which passage you use and which version of the Bible, it goes like this:

> Matthew 28:18-20 (NIV) – *Then Jesus came to them and said, "All authority in heaven and on earth has been given to me. Therefore go and make disciples of all nations, baptizing them in the name of the Father, and of the Son and of the Holy Spirit, and teaching them to obey everything I have commanded you. And surely I am with you always, to the very end of the age."*

Mark 16:15-18, 20 (NIV) – *He said to them, "Go into all the world and preach the good news to all creation. Whoever believes and is baptized will be saved, but whoever does not believe will be condemned. And these signs will accompany those who believe: In my name they will drive out demons; they will speak in new tongues; they will pick up snakes with their hands; and when they drink deadly poison, it will not hurt them at all; they will place their hands on sick people, and they will get well." Then the disciples went out and preached everywhere, and the Lord worked with them and confirmed his word by the signs that accompanied it.*

So ... is the "church" in America really doing it right? If so, are signs and wonders like this following? For the amount of time and money and people involved, we ought to be getting some really astounding miracles, right? Seems to me this is a guarantee.

IF Jesus wasn't kidding around, THEN He was just sure that if we did it HIS way there would be some surprising results. In America we are "evangelizing" all the time, but who are we reaching and what are we preaching? It would sure be a shame if we looked back and realized that we haven't really been doing it His way this whole time! What a waste of time, energy, money, lives and more importantly, souls, that would turn out to be! Seems like we ought to take every precaution to make sure we're on track.

I find that sometimes it's helpful to point out the reverse of an argument. For example: "IF dogs are man's best friend - and cats are not dogs, THEN cats are not man's best friend." Or like this: "Jesus never lied, so IF Jesus said big things would happen when we went out in His name - and big things aren't happening, THEN maybe we're not going out in His name."

Hmmm. Could that be? Are we preaching another Jesus? He said that if we loved Him and we were OF Him we would obey all His commandments - the last and greatest of which was the Great Commission. It's not the "Get- Around-To-It-Eventually Commission" or the "Leftover-10%-of-Budget Commission" or the "Somebody-Else-Can-Do-It Commission". It's the GREAT Commission and it applies to EVERY individual. There is no escape clause, there are no loopholes, there is no avoiding it and still claiming to be a Christ-like Christian if you ignore it and don't obey His command.

Maybe we're not doing it right. Should at least be worthy of some serious discussion, right? I mean, just if you want to please God and keep from being a Goat at the final judgement.

Here are some things that Jesus NEVER said to do:

- Go into all the world and build big buildings.

- Go into all the world and entertain the Christians.

- Go into all the world and ask the world for money.

- Go divide up into factions and constantly argue with each other.

- Go find people you can pay to go into all the world so you don't have to tell anyone yourself.

- Go into all the world that's easy to get to and will let you in without too much hassle.

- Go and elevate certain men above all the others and listen to them more than you listen to Me.

- Go into all the world and set up really excellent child-care programs.

- Go into all the world and see what you can learn from them about how to influence people.

- Go into all the world and identify the target demographic segment that will grow your church the fastest and then just focus on them.

- Go into all the world and find out what their gods have in common with your God and play to that.

- Go get an education so you'll be thoroughly prepared by the theories and programs of Man before you go do what Jesus commanded.

- Go into all the world and use sports leagues and antique car shows as a "low-impact" outreach tool.

- Go into all the world and build relationships for years before you can figure out how to work into a conversation the hard truth about their sinfulness and need for repentance.

- Go into all the world and preach the Tithe and that the people are stealing from God if they don't give you their 10%. (So you can spend it on things on this list.)

- Go into all the world and make as much money as you can so that you can give it to the Pastors and Priests and then you'll be blessed for your faith.

- Go into all the world and ignore all the poor people, recruit all the rich people, and then spend 90+% of all the revenue on yourself and your own comforts. Oh, and let people inside your organization steal 5%. (see Scary Stats)

- Go into all the world and learn to be just like them.

- Go into all the world and put them under "Law" instead of "Grace".

Maybe it's time we started doing it HIS way for a change.

Quick Thought

Our Father, who art in heaven, hallowed be Thy Name.

Thy kingdom come, thy will be done,

on earth as it is in heaven.

Give us this day our daily bread.

And forgive us our trespasses as we

forgive those who trespass against us.

And lead us not into temptation,

but deliver us from evil.

For thine is the kingdom and the

power and the glory, forever.

Amen.

We want His kingdom to come, right?

And we want what happens in heaven to happen on earth, right?

So ... how many <u>denominations</u> are there in heaven?

I don't think we could even have denominations if we were forgiving trespasses.

We must have been praying this wrong because His will isn't being done, our daily bread depends on bank loans, we're not forgiving trespasses and He's probably not forgiving US. We're certainly being tempted and I think we've been delivered TO evil - on a silver platter.

Oh! Maybe this is where it happened! Somebody in the church must be praying:

Mine is the Kingdom, Mine is the Power, Mine is the Glory, forever.

That could be it. I'm pretty sure God isn't happy about this. Could we stop it now?

Maybe say we're sorry? That'd be nice.

HUMAN SACRIFICE IN THE CHRISTIAN CHURCH

In the Old Testament there are lots of stories about the followers of Baal or Marduk or one god or another offering human sacrifices (and how unhappy about it Jehovah gets). Sometimes to please their gods so that they would have a good harvest or some other reason related to a hope for prosperity or blessing. They would get a virgin (or a baby) and sacrifice them on a stone altar in the hopes of some future comfort. They didn't lie about it. Everybody knew that was the plan. Even the virgin. At least the prophets of Baal had the decency to tell the virgin what they were doing and why. Maybe they even thanked her and threw a party before spilling her blood. That would be nice.

In America, the Christian church (as a whole) is much less honest. You see, we are saying that we care for the sick and poor and unreached, but what we're actually doing with our time and resources shows that we mean the exact opposite of that. We're knowingly letting them die so that we can have bounty and be comfy. And since we say we love them and we care about their eternal souls, not just their body, our insulting double-talk is amazingly more offensive! We average just 2% in giving and of that money ($250 Billion), we spend over 95% of it on ourselves. Less than 0.01% reaches the most unreached.

That's why the World is really irritated with us, because we're telling them we care and then we're spending our money on ourselves. Go read the Scary Stats again. Everything is exactly upside down of what we would be doing if we REALLY cared for those whom Jesus cared for most.

Put another way, in order for us to maintain our lush lifestyles (individually and as churches) we have to short-change God THEN we have to divert even the bulk of THAT back to ourselves as well.

Maybe a little parable will help. Jesus seemed to like those.

> Imagine your only child has a tumor. He's just a little kid, say seven years old. He's in the hospital, he's in a lot of pain, he's hooked up to all these machines, he desperately needs treatment, but it's going to cost $250,000 and you don't have any insurance. You, your wife and your friends and family help out and donate money, maybe you even have a telethon. It's a good thing that he looks good in the pictures, because that really helps. People all over are praying for you and sending their $10 and $20 bills in to help. They can just sense from your passion that that this is critically important to you to save this beautiful kid that you love so much. Tears are shed by all. You really mean well and it's all pure and sacrificial.

> And it turns out you meet your goal!! The full $250,000 is provided!

But then something inside snaps. Probably because of the big pile of cash you are completely unused to. So you take 95% off the top as administrative costs and go buy a fancy new car, a chandelier, new cushions for your furniture, new carpet, maybe build onto the house, get some new suits -- and you hand the doctors $12,500. Well it turns out that wasn't nearly enough, so you decide to keep raising money until that 5% can add up to the $250,000 you need to save his life. So at that rate, you're going to have to raise $5,000,000 to keep him alive. So you go back out with your plea for more money. You raise up more volunteers, take more pictures of him, maybe testimonials about how the people that helped him feel so good about themselves, maybe you spend a little more money jazzing up the materials you're mailing out. Shoot, you might even hire a consultant. And your wife is getting REALLY good at crying on cue.

At first you try not to make a big deal about all the stuff you bought because you don't want to have to explain it to people. But after a while you get this great new idea. If you tell them that the money you spent on yourself is God's evidence that you are blessed, then you can assert more strongly that they should support you so that THEY can share in YOUR blessing. I know it sounds completely crazy ... but you know, it just might work. People are greedy and selfish and they don't always see the big picture. Namely that it's THEIR money you're being blessed with and your kid is still getting sicker.

I mean, it's clear to everyone that he's in immediate danger and you're not. At some point, folks are going to start catching on because it's fairly likely that if you're this far down that road, you're going to just get more and more over the top. It's just a matter of time until you get your own jet plane and buy more houses for yourself and a stretch limousine and spend thousands on clothes and jewelry. Why not? I mean, this thing might go on forever if you can just reach enough people that haven't already figured it out. And if it happens that your kid dies because you never do get him the money, well that just makes you even more pitiful and brings more sympathy (that is, cash). Then you can go find somebody else's kid that's in the hospital and try it again. Now you're an "advocate."

At some point you start to wonder how this would play in other countries. Even if they don't have as much money, it's just a math problem - just a matter of how many people you can get to listen. I mean there are suckers all over the world. Why not give it a try?

So, what about the kid? Can you call that anything other than human sacrifice? Who's responsible for his death? The parents? Surely. There will be much darkness and crying and gnashing of teeth at the final judgement. But what about the people that sent in money? Surely they were just taken for a ride. It can't be THEIR fault. Except that, there is that part about how we're supposed to be good stewards of our money and give without thought of receiving. A lot of those folks sent in their money SO THAT they would be blessed financially. That can't possibly be a Biblically pure motive. Can it? I mean, it's not their fault they didn't ask any questions about how the money was being spent. Yeah, they were a little suspicious, but these are People of God up there on stage. They wouldn't rip us off, would they? I mean, they've got a best selling book out.

Oh, I'm sorry, you're not a part of that whole craziness? You saw right through those guys on the first try? You're just Joe Average American going to a nice quiet church and doing the right things? OK, well, let's try this. How much of your stuff do you think belongs to God? I mean, if you say He's LORD and all, that should mean He's the Master and King and you owe

123

Him everything, right? OK, so how are you spending God's money personally?

Odds are pretty good you're spending about 50% of your income on discretionary products - stuff you didn't absolutely need. God's not asking you to starve to death. He loves us and wants us to be happy and content, but He's not really after making us fat and lazy. Where's all that stuff you're buying coming from? What did it take to get it to you at the low, low, one-time only sale prices you paid for it. (I mean, you did shop around, right?)

Ever consider this? Revelation 18:10-13 (ESV)

"Alas! Alas! You great city, you mighty city, Babylon! For in a single hour your judgment has come." And the merchants of the earth weep and mourn for her, since no one buys their cargo anymore, cargo of gold, silver, jewels, pearls, fine linen, purple cloth, silk, scarlet cloth, all kinds of scented wood, all kinds of articles of ivory, all kinds of articles of costly wood, bronze, iron and marble, cinnamon, spice, incense, myrrh, frankincense, wine, oil, fine flour, wheat, cattle and sheep, horses and chariots, and slaves, that is, human souls."

Get it? Do you know what it COSTS for merchants around the world to get that stuff made and bring it here? It costs HUMAN SOULS. How many are having the life sucked out of them in factories around the world so that we can have STUFF? Children, prisoners, widows - Christians in prison even! Ever think of that? That you might go buy a "Made in China" bible cover or cross necklace and it's being made by Chinese pastors in prison who have to work 16 hour days making stuff like that in order to earn dinner? That's just the kind of thing the enemy would have them doing, too. It's happening. Don't think it's not.

Think hard. Are you sure this is what Christ wanted? I mean it's all His stuff right? Or did you not mean "Lord" that way? How many questions are you asking?

THE BOTTOM LINE

"Command those who are rich in this present world not to be arrogant nor to put their hope in wealth, which is so uncertain, but to put their hope in God, who richly provides us with everything for our enjoyment. Command them to do good, to be rich in good deeds, and to be generous and willing to share. In this way they will lay up treasure for themselves as a firm foundation for the coming age, so that they may take hold of the life that is truly life." - I Tim. 6:21

If you want to put your finger on what's wrong with the church in American today, just follow the money. Always follow the money.

See ... God gave a businessman a successful business and much money. God gave the man savvy and shrewdness and management skills. God taught him how to be a good steward and build something strong. God placed him in a church where he could contribute his talents and skills.

Then ... the businessman checked his brain at the door and handed over all his treasure to those LEAST educated and trained in the management of money. They have no experience with it and it's potential dangers. But they've got a seminary degree. So before you know it, they offer to let the businessman put his name on the new wing, they spend his money like crazy on any fool program that looks like fun and their other pastor buddies are doing, and if they're really lucky and play by the rules, they get offered a chance to go do the same stuff at a church with twice as many businessmen.

Who is God going to hold most responsible? Clearly the pastor is guilty for not leading the sheep correctly and maybe even for harming them and being prideful. But to some degree he's just doing what he was trained to do and learned in seminary.

But the businessman was given many gifts and he didn't ask ANY of the questions he had been trained to ask of a business venture looking to spend his capital. He didn't ask about Return On Investment or look to cut back or contain costs like he would in his own business. Particularly if you're trying to be Christ-like. The largest waste of useable space in this country is all the big buildings being used a few hours a day, twice a week!

Businessmen didn't go to seminary, but they can interpret the model of Christ and his hope for us same as anyone else. Businessmen should be able to prioritize and meet urgent needs and problem-solve and be entrepreneurial – or at least think about risk-management. But they haven't been, even though they're Chairman of the Deacons and head of the Finance Committee (all worldly structures, by the way). Mostly they've just been checking their brains at the door for years.

I think consciously or subconsciously the reason American Christians only tithe 2% is because they know that if they were obedient and gave FIVE times as much there would be gold plated mega churches on every corner and every pastor would have his own TV show. There'd be Jesus theme parks in every big town. Everything EXCEPT raw, effective evangelism and care for those in most need.

I can't begin to tell you how badly we've managed the money. It's awful, AWFUL! Horrifyingly bad. I'm still just trying to get my head around how bad it is. It's no wonder the secular world hates us. We're all hypocrites of the highest order. More than any other part of the church anywhere ever! The Catholic Church during the Inquisition wasn't as bad! For what we could have been with our blessings, we've let hundreds of millions of souls go to hell and millions of Brothers and Sisters starve to death. So that we could have padded pews and new carpet.

I know of one Evangelical church (that believes in the imminent return of Christ) with a chandelier that cost $1,000,000!! The pastor didn't pay for it out of HIS pocket! It was the folks with the big money that played along. They're going to have to account for the decisions they made as stewards of God's blessings. When they "stand" before Jesus to account they're going to be wishing they could get UNDER the ground.

I'm telling you flat out, the folks that did the worst damage need to be crushed - and then they need to go see to it that the church changes it's ways. Look at it the other way - if you DON'T get the businessman to repent, he'll see to it that they find another pastor before he'll give up the shiny buildings he donated.

Until they are a great crushing weight pressing against the souls of the guilty, the massive piles of money in this country will not be liberated to go be a blessing to the unreached, the widows, and the orphans as we're commanded. We'll never live according the the model of Jesus and we'll always be hypocrites. There's going to be some serious heart-crying when this message finally sinks in. We have a lot to atone for.

Clear enough?

(Luke 12:13-21, Luke 14:8-14, James 5:1-6, I Timothy 6, I Corinthians 4:6-21, 2 Corinthians 8:1-15, 2 Corinthians 9:6-15, and more!)

Musical Interlude - Feel free to sing along

ALL to Jesus I surrender; **ALL** to him I freely give;

I will ever love and trust him, in his presence daily live.

I surrender **ALL**, I surrender **ALL**,
ALL to thee, my blessed Savior, I surrender **ALL**.

ALL to Jesus I surrender; humbly at his feet I bow,

worldly pleasures **ALL** forsaken; take me, Jesus, take me now.

I surrender **ALL**, I surrender **ALL**, **ALL** to thee, my blessed
Savior, I surrender **ALL**.

ALL to Jesus I surrender; make me, Savior, wholly thine;

fill me with thy love and power; truly know that thou art mine.

I surrender **ALL**, I surrender **ALL**,
ALL to thee, my blessed Savior, I surrender **ALL**.

ALL to Jesus I surrender; now I feel the sacred flame.

O the joy of full salvation! Glory, glory, to his name!

I surrender **ALL**, I surrender **ALL**,
ALL to thee, my blessed Savior, I surrender **ALL**.

What EXACTLY did you think "ALL" meant?

Read Matt 22:37, Mark 12:30, Luke 10:27.

That's a lot of "ALL's"!

How about Proverbs 3:5-6.

"Lean not on your own understanding but in ALL your ways acknowledge Him and HE will direct your paths."

Which part of your own understand should you keep leaning on?

How much 'joy of full salvation' and 'sacred flame' do you get to feel if you surrender SOME?

Who do you think you're lying to?

He knows the difference.

You can't hide from God!

Read Acts 5:1-11.

Ananias and Saphira said 'ALL' and meant 'Some'.

Very bad idea. Very bad.

Next time, sing it like you mean it ALL the way.

Or you might just drop dead for surrendering SOME.

BREAD AND CIRCUSES

I've long been aware of this and what it means and how satan uses it to take over a culture. America has been substantially co-opted already by this ancient Roman strategy. In fact, I think it predates Rome since it's a ploy of the enemy and you can see evidence of it being used to destroy cultures and distract people all the way back to the Garden of Eden.

Here are some references so you can look it up on your own.

This phrase originates in Satire X of the Roman poet Juvenal of the late 1st and early 2nd centuries CE. In context, the Latin phrase *panem et circenses* (bread and circuses) is given as the only remaining cares of a Roman populace which has given up its birthright of political freedom:

.. Already long ago, from when we sold our vote to no man, the People have abdicated our duties; for the People who once upon a time handed out military command, high civil office, legions - everything, now restrains itself and anxiously hopes for just two things: **bread and circuses**   (Juvenal, Satire 10.77-81)

Juvenal here makes reference to the elite Roman practice of providing free wheat to some poor Romans as well as costly circus games and other forms of entertainment as a means gaining political power through popularity. The Dictionary of Cultural Literacy (1993) states that Juvenal displayed his contempt for the declining heroism of his contemporary Romans in this passage. Spanish intellectuals between the 19th and 20th centuries complained about the similar *pan y toros* ("bread and bull[fight]s").
(http://en.wikipedia.org/wiki/Bread_and_circuses)

The American Heritage® Dictionary of the English Language (Fourth Edition. 2000) defines "bread and circuses" as a plural noun meaning "Offerings, such as benefits or entertainments, intended to placate discontent or distract attention from a policy or situation.
http://www.bartleby.com/61/39/B0463950.html

There was a day before God scrubbed it all out of me that I was quite the political junkie and conspiracy theory nut. In that age, I watched Bill O"Reilly regularly. I didn't remember it, but when I did a web search on this topic, this artice that he wrote for World Net Daily came up. It illustrates the situation in America pretty well.
http://www.worldnetdaily.com/news/article.asp?ARTICLE_ID=21781

I'm not writing this as a condemnation of America – it is Rome and it does what Rome does, which is dumb down the populace by keeping them entertained, protecting the food supply and making sure they feel safe and patriotic. That way, they won't notice that the whole Empire is crumbling around them and a small number of elites are running the show without oversight or accountability.

Only 50% of America has enough motivation to get up off their sofas once every four years and vote for president! I hope you can understand that by feeding us an endless stream of NFL and NASCAR and WWE Wrestling and thousands of cable stations and porn and video games and concerts and cell phones and the internet and endless diversions and holidays and parades and games, we are left in a state of such continuous motion and input overload that we never can focus on the important things. And as long as there is food and drink on the shelves at the grocery store, the TV works and most of the people we know have jobs, why worry? We're the greatest nation on earth. What could happen? We're the only super power left, right?

Was that condemning? I didn't really mean it to be, that's just the "world" being the "world" and doing what it does – which is obey satan.

I've long seen the application of this and the danger of it and the insidious way it which it distracts people and is used as part of the dangerous dialectic drumbeat to get our focus away from the important things. Americans are suckers for "bread and circuses". Can there be any doubt?

Here's the real point of this writing.

One day, I'm just minding my own business, driving in the car and God just plops this phrase into my head.

"Bread and circuses."

"OK, yeah, I know what that is, Lord, what's the point?"

"That's what the church is doing."

Then it just all hit me like a giant tidal wave and I almost slammed on the brakes. As I recall, I pulled over to the shoulder of the highway in tears.

"OH! GOD!!! They TOTALLY ARE!! They totally are! It's all about the shows and the food!! They're keeping them entertained, engaging them in so many things so fast that they can't slow down. They're keeping them fat and comfy so they won't notice that they are blind and naked and wretched and poor! Oh, God! I'm so sorry! Please forgive us! We're not really addressing their spirit at all, just their brain and their body! They can't slow down long enough to even pray! Please forgive us. Please fix it. Please crush that out of Your true church. Please make them stop! Oh, my God! I'm so sorry!"

And on like that for about a half hour until He told me to stop. Lots of crying when it all crystallized. I have understood for a long time how devastatingly dangerous this strategy is and how it can totally co-opt a nation, but I'd never made the leap and seen how the enemy of our souls had inserted it so thoroughly into the whole of the church of America. Can there be any doubt? Are we not the most overstimulated, overfed, spiritually starving people on the planet? Even getting a church member to slow down long enough to be introspective about the true state of their soul and their salvation is a miracle in itself!

We told them that they were saved and safe – their Roman citizenship is secure – either because they said a little prayer or they prayed the Rosary enough times or because their name is on the roles of our denomination and they're tithing.

"There are no worries now! You're safe! Now come for dinner on Wednesday night and fellowship with us. Bring a pie. And don't miss the Christmas cantata! We have a real, live baby camel! And here's a sign-up sheet for the softball league. And the senior adults are taking a bus trip together to go shopping in Amish country next month. OH! And the youth are going on a mission trip to Cancun during Spring Break. And if you call now you can register for our special "Jesus Cruise" around the Carribean – we're going to have several major Christian celebrities and musicians there that you might get to actually touch! Maybe you could even sit with Michael W. Smith and eat from the 500 item buffet!! We might even have a baby camel on the ship! Oh, you just HAVE to come! God will be so pleased if you can make it."

It's all bread and circuses. And it's all from the enemy of our souls. How can I tell? Because if God were really in charge, we would be like Jesus and we'd all be on our faces crying until we sweat blood for the horrible state of things and a clear vision of the cup that has been and will be poured out on us before we get through this. We'd be weeping and repenting in sackcloth and ashes for the missed opportunities and millions (or billions) of souls that have been lost while we entertained ourselves and got fatter and fatter. If God was in charge, we would have Fear of the Lord and we would cry until we ran out of tears for the mess we've made of His Body. We'd sincerely apologize to the "world" because we had the Light that they needed, but we blew it out so that we could become just like them. Even while we kept telling them we were "different."

If God was in charge of the "church," He'd take a flamethrower to our structures and our systems and our programs and our leaders and our own lives and burn off all the chaff instead of catering to it. He'd turn over the tables and cleanse the temple. (And I think that's coming, so you might want to pray real hard.)

Hmmm. I don't think we can put Him off forever. I wonder when that's gonna start? Now would be nice.

If you have the guts, pray this with me:

Father God, I know we have dishonored You in ways I can't even get my head around. I know that you can't possibly be happy with our fancy shows that just entertain our own brain, but leave people untransformed for the Gospel and dead in their sins. Please make the "bread and circuses" stop by whatever means necessary. I'm sorry for the mess I've made of my life, my home, my city, my nation, the Bride. Please, Lord, please bring a flamethrower to all of it. Please wreck it all. Anything that stands in the way between me and You, please do whatever it takes.

Rip it, tear it, shred it, kill it, crush it, burn it – if I can't lay it down then just snatch it out of my grip. For the structures and systems that I've helped build, I repent. Wreck them all. Have Your way. Use what You can and flatten the rest. Please, Father, let NO ONE stand in front of Your sheep anymore and say, "Mine is the kingdom, Mine is the power, Mine is the glory." If they're not going to repent, then take them home. You know who can be redeemed, but make them sit down and shut up and weep and mourn – or take them home. There is so much blood on their head already, it's just mercy to make it stop. Do whatever You have to do to me so that I'll be a useful vessel for Your kingdom, broken and contrite and circumcised of heart. Teach me humility and give me more Fear of the Lord. Please pour out a gift of repentance on me by Your Holy Spirit so that I can cry rivers of tears in front of anybody until this thing turns around. Please let me see through Your eyes and share in Your suffering. I'm so sorry, Lord. Please do it. I trust You. Make me useful. Turn this around! In the mighty Name of Jesus Christ my Lord. Amen.

And don't stop praying until things change.

WHAT IS THE PROPER USE OF FUNDS?

Based on: Luke 12:13-21, Luke 14:8-14, James 5:1-6,

I Timothy 6, I Corinthians 4:6-21, 2 Corinthians 8:1-15, 2 Corinthians 9:6-15, and more!

If you have ten credit cards maxed out and you want to pay them off, you start by paying off the ones with the largest interest rate first, right? Then you move up the chain to the ones that don't hurt as bad until you get them all paid off. If you have one at 0% interest, you don't mess with it at all, if you don't have to.

God's math works the same way. The plan for us should be to go help those in the most need first (permanent, eternal need and tragic, immediate physical needs). In America the average person gets an offer or opportunity to hear about the Gospel over 500 times per year. In many countries, a person may have a 10 minute window ONCE in their whole life to hear the Good News. Over a billion people have never even once heard the name of Jesus spoken in their presence. Every year millions die without Christ. In America, no one can say they never had a chance.

In terms of poverty, the poor in the U.S. live like kings compared to the devastatingly poor in Delhi and Burma and Haiti and a thousand other places. They would love to trade places with our poor! No one can statistically argue otherwise with any honesty. Especially if you've seen it first-hand. Where would you rather be a girl and be an orphan? China, Burma, Iran, India? Or Canada, USA, England?

So whether it's their eternal soul or their physical body, logic says that first and foremost you care for the worst off - and then (in order) you help the Very Poor, the Somewhat Poor, the Poor, the Slightly Uncomfortable – and you NEVER spend a dime on the Got-More-Than-Anyone-Could-Ever-Really-Need-But-Still-Dissatisfied!

Then those reached can be an example of success and maybe they can even help as we move up to reach those in the next category. There are lots of devastatingly, oppressively poor churches that are sending out missionaries and being obedient with what little they have. Are we as good an example? At the rate they're going, it won't be long before China is sending their missionaries to the West.

Jesus had the largest heart for the most impoverished. He took the most care and attention with those rejected by the rest of the world. The Christian church in America has often done the exact opposite. In Revelations 2 and 3, Jesus speaks to the seven churches. He gives them an encouragement and then a rebuke -- except the poor churches of Smyrna and Philadelphia who were obedient despite limited resources. For them there is only blessing and no word of judgement. The worst judgement is against the rich church of Laodecia in Revelations 3. At the final call, which kind of church will Jesus judge yours to have been?

If we are to lust after and covet something, it should be treasure in Heaven where it can't rust or be eaten by moths or stolen by man. As for me, I want to see who is building the largest pile of Heavenly treasure and then I want to buy stock in them. I want to be a part of whatever they're doing and help any way I can. We're often told there are just two options; make lots of money and be controlled by it -or- make a tiny bit of money and learn to live simply. But there is another choice - make lots of money and live simply and then invest all the excess into the Kingdom. If God has blessed you with skills and assets and talents, use them. He's going to expect a report on how well you invested it so as to maximize your return in Heavenly treasure.

I mean, everything you have is all HIS right? When you said He was "Lord" you meant it, right? When you said "All" you really meant it, didn't you?

IS "CHURCH" REALLY GOING TO
PERSECUTE "<u>THE</u> CHURCH"?

Just in case you're new to all this stuff, we should probably define our terms. There is the organized structure of "religion" that most folks refer to as the "church" (or churches) and then there is the Biblical and pure Body of Christ that is the True Church. One is Man-made and the other is established by God and consists of those who are "called out." In the Greek it is called Ekklesia (or Ecclesia, in English). Certain subsets may overlap, but they ARE NOT interchangeable!

It should be clear from history that every major move of God (or even cultural change) is most ferociously opposed by the established religious structures themselves. I don't see how anyone can historically deny that. Besides it being the nature of Man to fight back when his comfort zone is assaulted.

Remember Judges 6-8 and the story of Gideon? Under cover of darkness he knocked down one altar to Baal and built on it's spot an altar to God and in the morning when everyone woke up, all the men of the tribe wanted to kill him. Sometimes it's just the shock of the change that freaks us out, not so much the right or wrong of the change itself. (One chapter later they want Gideon to be king and they convert all the rest of the altars in Israel.) But we need to expect that people don't like their boats rocked.

Let's just look at this from a purely pragmatic, financial standpoint.

The Bible says that the "love of money is the root of all evil." There's more discussion about money than almost anything else in the Bible. And almost all of it is warning us about it's dangers and pitfalls. Let's first approach the possibilities on a purely financial basis.

If you have any comprehension of what $250 BILLION dollars can do, you might begin to understand the market forces at work here. That's the annual income of the Church - not even including it's total asset value which is surely in the TRILLIONS! We've got giant denominational buildings and hospitals and retreat centers and mission boards and printing presses and lots and lots of paid staff. All that overhead requires stability, and preferably, constant growth.

If you start to do ANYTHING that would potentially threaten the income stream of certain segments of the "church," there will be all kinds of forces that will try to stop you. Consider this, Driftwood Super Church (for example) is building a giant new building. It is warm and soft and friendly and seeker sensitive. Everybody leaves feeling good. The pastor even has a best selling book and is on TV regularly. But members of the congregation start to wonder how much treasure in heaven they are really accumulating for all their investment into Driftwood. They begin to look down at their weekly check and realize that it would make more of an eternal difference on lives if they spent it on native missionaries and feeding the hungry and clothing the naked - instead of a new JumboTron and a fountain out front. So ... they keep coming to church but they give their money elsewhere to hyper-efficient organizations working on the front lines.

What if 10% of them got that thought in their head? The annual budget would come up five weeks short. Not only that, but you now have NON-PAYING customers taking up seats - using resources, flushing the toilets, talking to staff, using up bulletins, occupying parking spots, requiring volunteers to watch their kids. In essence you have doubled the damage of the revenue shortfall. You've withheld revenue AND you've kept a paying customer out of the seats. That shiny new pastor that keeps the seats filled by tickling everyone's ears starts looking a lot less shiny.

What if it's enough to stall a building campaign in progress? Now you've got Teamsters and construction workers mad at you. Shouldn't be surprising if some of those construction companies and banks are owned by the deacons and elders in the churches. With the massive debt load in most of our churches (another tip-off that there might be a structural problem here), maybe even banks have to start foreclosing. You've got chair suppliers, hymnal printers, sound system installers, roofers, stained glass artists, banner makers, architects and dozens of others who could stand to lose out.

What if Simon & Schuster's newest best-selling pastor/author starts to have trouble keeping his church out of hock? If there was an attitudinal and financial shift within the church - even 10% - that's a potential revenue loss of tens of millions for Sony, Viacom, Fox News, Time Warner and many other high power organizations.

And ... there are all kinds out there. If this is a war, you have to come to the conclusion that some of the "Christian" leaders are double-agents, because they're doing more harm than good. It's bad enough that you might be assaulted by people who love Jesus and are just shocked and surprised - but we also need to acknowledge that the forces of darkness are hard at work inside our own ranks and they are MUCH more ruthless. What response should you expect from some of the most egregious televangelist, Bentley-driving, crying all the time, gotta have money to stay on the air, taking pennies from widows, buy-a-miracle-for-yourdonation variety? They've got millions of dollars at their disposal and apparently very little morality to constrain them. How hard would it be for them to take you out?

And that's just barely scratching the surface of the macro-economics at play here.

What about the theological response? Since what we're advocating is a return to the pure Word of God and a commitment to listen to God only and let Him be our teacher - we are implicitly devaluing a seminary education and setting a level playing field among all who love Jesus. In fact, we're saying that it's entirely possible that a 13 year old girl or a guy fresh out of jail or a shut-in 90 year old widow might know Jesus better than a guy with a Doctorate. We didn't set out to devalue a seminary education, it's just that most of what they teach is man-made theory and not necessarily useful for hearing the voice of God better. (In fact, many church leaders will think you're nuts if you say you actually hear the voice of God and do what He tells you!)

By some accounts more than 60% of professional Christian clergy in this country do not believe the Bible is the inerrant word of God. So we're assaulting their sensibilities by trying to take it literally. They will say the idea of City Churches is impossible in today's world. They will insist that there are problems in the church but either; 1) THEIR denomination is not so bad, or 2) the Biblical solution (repent and act like One Body) is not the way to go. Nearly all of them will disagree with the premise that a paid clergy is unnecessary and/or unBiblical. The religious establishment will fight tooth and nail. They will call you a cult, they will warn their members against you, they will call all the other pastors they know, they will conduct media campaigns to run you out of town. I've talked to a lot of pastors about the "Apology to the World" and the Scary Stats and Scary Scriptures and the conclusions that I've come to. Many don't like it, some don't like me, some think I'm just disgruntled and mad at the church - but none of them have ever honestly argued about the theology or the scriptural validity or the veracity of the statistics. No one has ever shown me where in the Bible there are multiple churches in one town and God is happy about it. No one has ever shown me in the Bible where one person has a better pipeline of information to God than another so he should stand up front and everybody should sit quietly and listen to that guy talk once a week.

What about the personal response? Surely there will be people in the churches that see there is a problem with the output we are getting here, with the return-on-investment that we are seeing. Odds are good that the first ones to get it will be business professionals that run companies and know how to make a payroll and keep their books balanced. And odds are good people like that are already sitting on the Board (or Committee or Elders or whatever). These are high visibility, highly respected members that may start to react in visible and forceful ways to make things change. There are all kinds of interpersonal dynamics and relationships at risk here. Hurt feelings, betrayal, confrontation of all kinds may ensue. Without holiness of heart and a commitment to love unconditionally, the result could be depression, frustration, exhaustion, resignation or worse. And that doesn't even BEGIN to diagnose the possible responses from the "world" and government to a true New Testament Christianity spreading widely! What if all the Christians emptied their retirement accounts and gave it to the poor? Wouldn't the stock market melt down? THEN you'd see some real persecution!

Oh! And if persecution actually did start in America – if the day came when jack-booted storm troopers came to arrest all the Christians ... maybe we'll wish we had rethought the whole church-wide pictorial directory thing.

GEN-X – GEN-Y – ENVIRONMENTALISTS – ANARCHISTS – ATHEISTS

READ THIS!!

First off, we're REALLY, REALLY sorry! We're praying daily that we can get the church to be what it was always supposed to be so you won't see us anymore as the hypocrites we are. Just as in the fairy tale about the Emperor's New Clothes, it's youth that is willing to speak truth and is unconstrained by convention and possessions. That's why Jesus blessed the little ones and encouraged us to have faith as a child. As it turns out, faith like a thoughtful, steady, mature, settled adult who has enmeshed themselves in sinful culture is disastrous for the church!!

We firmly believe that whatever this is to become will be dependent on the GenX/Y'ers and their energy, enthusiasm, computer savvy, and willingness to take a stand. We have always sent young people to fight our wars.

So does God (Daniel, Joseph, David, John the Baptist, Jesus, and on and on through the ages).

Your generation has a very hard time going into a giant fancy building and listening to guys in suits and seeing big musical productions - where people leave unmoved and unchanged. You don't need that stuff to find God and you think it's frivolous and wasteful. And you're absolutely right. Instead of trying to strategically cater to you with a new "twist" on old church - we're advocating the complete renewal of the church to its roots. Which just happens to be exactly what you're calling for.

Your generation has been raised up by God to throw off the status quo and the old assumptions. It's not enough to do it this way because that's what we've always done. You need to go back to the basics, to the very heart and core of what the message of Jesus is all about. You have been raised to respect nature, to recycle and reuse, to embrace people of different colors and languages, to rage against "the machine." Those in the Big Church establishments think "the machine" is government and corporations, but it's not just that. It's not just Big Government, Big Tobacco, Big Oil, Big Pharmaceuticals - it's Big Church that stands condemned as well.

I absolutely believe that Satan has built educational systems to get our children focused on all the wrong things, to worship the creation rather than the Creator (Romans 1:25). To worship Mother Earth instead of He who made the whole of creation. To worship the stars and constellations instead of He who hung them. To value human justice and equality, instead of looking to He who yearns for it more than any of us – and sent the Word (Jesus) to achieve it and the Holy Spirit to constantly urge us toward it.

But the joke is on Satan. Jesus is the ultimate expression of stewardship, recycling, care for the poor and disadvantaged, love for those different, respect for nature and the beauty of Creation. You've been perfectly prepared - by the Enemy - for what's coming! Your very souls resonate and vibrate at a different pitch from the current Church structures. Something big is on the horizon. A complete revolution in our relationship to God and the expression of Christianity. Many of you could feel it before we did. I pray that we who have influence and should have known better than to let it get this bad can change quickly enough that we don't lose all of you forever.

To the Anarchists among you - God bless you. You almost get it! Human structures and hierarchies and organizational charts are blasphemous to the very nature and spirit of God Almighty. God wants us in constant communion with His Spirit and under the sole direction of His will. No layers are needed if we're in harmony with God. It won't be the disordered chaos that you picture it to be - God's is the ultimate expression of process and order - He just doesn't need man-made organizational structures. The day is coming when Christ will reign on a glorified and perfected Earth in exactly that way. No layers, no structures - just us and God. Please think carefully about the difference between the Created and the Creator. The beauty and complexity of nature is not the end, it's the glorious sign along the way that was created to point to a loving, beautiful, complex God. DON'T let yourself get sucked into any big, complex human structures - not the Church as it currently is and especially not a One-World government designed by sinful, imperfect man!

God sent His very own son, Jesus - a young radical intent on calling the people back to their core and to restore their pure love for God (John 3:16-17) - even though speaking against the establishment was to carry the cost of the most horrible imaginable torture and death. He came to redeem us of our sinful nature and offer us an opportunity to plug into the One True Song.

Tell your friends! There are "grown-ups" that get it! God has a plan and YOU'RE at the front lines! Change is coming! Be a part of the solution!

We don't want your money. We don't want anybody's money. We want you to worship God. We want you to hear His Voice and be led by Him only. We want the "Big Church" to repent of its sinfulness and return to a love of God above all. The time of the worship of money is coming to an end.

Praise God for using a helpless worm like me and offering His Son as a sacrifice to redeem my sinfulness so that He could adopt us and make us all joint heirs with Jesus. Change is coming! There are going to be some people really, REALLY unhappy about having to give up all their stuff.

It's going to be a fun ride!

Musical Interlude -
Feel free to sing along

Zacchaeus was a wee little man, a wee little man was he,

He climbed up in the sycamore tree, The Savior for to see.

And when the Savior passed that way,
He looked up in the tree,

And He said, "Zacchaeus, you come down,
For I'm going to your house today,

For I'm going to your house today."

Zacchaeus was a wee little man, a wee little man was he,

He climbed up in the sycamore tree, The Savior for to see.

And Zacchaeus came down from that tree,

And He said, "What a better man I'll be.
I'll give my money to the poor.

What a better man I'll be.
What a better man I'll be."

I wonder if we've been
leaving out that last verse?

I sure don't remember hearing it lately.

When did we stop singing <u>that</u> verse?

THE SPIRIT OF ABORTION

I've been praying for a single coherent nugget to explain the problem and God showed it to me a few days ago.

It is the VERY ESSENCE and CORE of what God did for us! He sent Jesus to shepherd us and be an example and then God ADOPTED us as joint heirs with Jesus. It is the supreme and ULTIMATE example and pure essence of love to take someone that you KNOW has problems and special needs and sinfulness, that you KNOW will require effort and cost - even the awful sacrifice of your own blood Son - and then elevate this stranger to the status equal to the Son of your womb. Equal to the Morning Star in inheritance and love. OK, yeah, we all know that, but do you REALLY GET IT?!

One of the things that many of us have been praying for is that a Spirit of Adoption would sweep over the church and the world. God finally just put all the pieces together in my head. This is why we're adopting a kid from China, this is why God had me build a company that brings in people and THEN asks them what they'd like to do here and loves them and refuses to lay them off. That's why I'm mad at the Church Growth Movement and mega churches that don't seem to care.

Do you get it? A Christian company that lays off people that are supposed to be part of the family is ABORTING them! They're expensive or inconvenient or not playing along with our plan. Do you really think Jesus is going to be proud of a Christian business that is INDISTINGUISHABLE from a secular one? If not THIS to differentiate us - then what?

Churches that urge you out because they don't like dealing with you are ABORTING YOU! For all our talk about being against abortion, that's just physical. Those babies are NOT in spiritual, eternal danger. But when we "urge" someone out of our churches, we're potentially aborting their souls! Do you honestly think Jesus is going to say, "Well, you aborted this person out of your church and they grew to hate religion and never prayed to me again, but I understand, it's OK. You know, they WERE kind of weird and smelly and didn't really fit in with the rest of us up here." Maybe they asked hard questions, maybe they didn't tithe like we thought they should, maybe they never even got in the door because we made it clear we were better than them. How can you call it anything BUT the Spirit of Abortion?

I think businesses that do family-friendly programs just to improve retention or improve profitability aren't Families anymore, they're ORPHANAGES. They're just warehousing people and trying to keep them efficient and not revolt!

Churches that warehouse as many people as possible to get the subsidy per person that comes, are ORPHANAGES! Of course, they still SAY they're a family and love everyone, but people can sense that at a certain point it changed and now it's really about numbers. Somewhere off in a remote corner they have a Dying Room where they just let the troubled ones anguish and wither. A church that feeds the children pablum to keep them under-nourished and not growing is suppressing them because toddlers are much easier to warehouse than rebellious teenagers! How much love does that show? How much Spirit of Adoption is that?

It's like Xin Guang, the little girl with special needs that we are going to pick up in China (God willing) around Easter {2005, now home! But ended up July.} and for whom God has told us we're to be her "Forever Family." It's like if we just decided she was so cute at three years old that we'd like to keep her like that, so we reduce her meal portions and then get her hooked on coffee and cigarettes to stunt her growth so she'll stay just that size forever. Because we hear teenage girls are too much trouble. What kind of love would that show?! And what of our bio-daughter and the lessons she learns from that? Don't you think Family Services would come and snatch them BOTH away and throw us in jail?! Well, that's what's about to happen to the churches acting that way! And Christian businesses are not going to be exempt either.

That's why house churches work - if they can keep their focus. They're small enough and intimate enough to maintain that Spirit. That's why MILLIONS of us have left the institutional church entirely, because we sense that that Spirit of Adoption is GONE and we don't know where to find it except in communion with God directly! By it's nature it's TREMENDOUSLY difficult for a large autocratic organism to maintain a personal intimate Spirit of Adoption. This sweet, wonderful Spirit of Unconditional Love is the ultimate enemy of Satan, because he was offered it by God and rejected it and hates anyone who accepts it or encourages it or models it! Get it?

That's IT! That's the core of it all!

Thanks be for the Word of the Lord and for His willingness to come show us what true LOVE means!! Thanks be to God for being the Spirit of Adoption without which we would be lost forever!! Praise God!! Thanks be to God for giving us a chance to be living examples of His love for us.

Test your hearts. Test your family. Test your church. Test your business. Is the Spirit of Adoption foremost? It is UNDENIABLY the ROOT of LOVE and your best chance to manifestly express through your lives that you ARE Christian and you DO understand your responsibilities as Adopted Children of God. The ultimate sign to Satan that you are DANGEROUS to his cause is the evidence in your life of this Spirit of Adoption and a willingness to sacrifice ANYTHING for those entrusted to your family. I want to be at the very top of Satan's hit list. Praise God! What about you?

Hold on tight, folks. When people really GET this, it's all going to start moving FAST! A New Song is coming!

Musical Interlude - Sing along

When we walk with the Lord in the light of His Word,
What a glory He sheds on our way!

While we do His good will, He abides with us still,
And with all who will trust and obey.

Trust and obey, for there's no other way
To be happy in Jesus, but to trust and obey.

Not a shadow can rise, not a cloud in the skies,
But His smile quickly drives it away;

Not a doubt or a fear, not a sigh or a tear,
Can abide while we trust and obey.

Trust and obey, for there's no other way
To be happy in Jesus, but to trust and obey.

Not a burden we bear, not a sorrow we share,
But our toil He doth richly repay;

Not a grief or a loss, not a frown or a cross,
But is blessed if we trust and obey.

Trust and obey, for there's no other way
To be happy in Jesus, but to trust and obey.

Then in fellowship sweet we will sit at His feet.
Or we'll walk by His side in the way.

What He says we will do, where He sends we will go;
Never fear, only trust and obey.

Trust and obey, for there's no other way
To be happy in Jesus, but to trust and obey.

TEN COMMANDMENTS – HOW DOES THE "CHURCH" STACK UP?

If there is no real persecution of Christians in America and Jesus said the more you are like Him the more you will be persecuted, then there must not be very many real Christians in America. See any logic problems there? Did you think Jesus was kidding?

So ... my goal is to bring persecution as quickly as possible by saying whatever I have to say to get Christians to start fully and completely acting like Christ. That will require lots of people who are willing to fearlessly take a stand and STOP CONFORMING TO THE WORLD. I've been blowing the trumpet and a few have gathered, but then I didn't have the lung capacity and wisdom I have now - and probably the willingness to do what it takes. I think the time is coming when somebody is going to blow the trumpet REALLY loud. If not me then someone else. Probably LOTS of people.

There's a fire burning in me that is just getting hotter. Some stuff is coming out of me right now that is so harsh that I need folks with lots of love around me to temper it. We have to keep it about love first, but still say the hard things when necessary.

For example, it occurs to me that the "church" as we know it has a personality, dysfunctional and disjointed as it is, it has certain trends and behaviors that you could define as a personality. I've done a lot of work in the area of organizational theory and believe that groups have a personality that can be defined and diagnosed. Maybe the same methods you would use to convict and witness to an individual would work on a group.

Anyway, that which we call 'church', if it is really off track according to God's Law, should be showing bad fruit. Using Ray Comfort's method of showing people their sinfulness using the Ten Commandments, let's take a look. (And understand this is HIGHLY abbreviated, we could write a book on the stats and examples for each one!)

Worship no other gods before me.

Comfy, Sunday-only Jesus is NOT the same God. Purpose-Driven Jesus is NOT the same God of our Fathers! Worshiping the pastor because he has a book deal or worshiping the denomination, structure, money, or even ideology (Calvin, KJV 1611, Pope) is putting other gods before HIM. **GUILTY!**

Do not make idols or worship them.

Your heart is where you spend your time and money. According to the stats, the Western church loves themselves and their buildings and comforts most of all. We spend many times more hours worshiping TV than we do God Almighty. We cancel Sunday services to watch the Super Bowl, for Pete's sake! **GUILTY!**

Do not use the name of your God irreverently or in vain.

To justify ANY stupid thing we want to do, we assure people that we can be trusted since we hear from God. Touch not God's anointed! Whatever just came out of this or that pastor or prophet's mouth must have been the voice of God - they have a new DVD out and speak at conferences all over the world! We have pastors, bishops, popes that stand in for God and speak on His behalf - with or without His approval - taking His Name and authority as their own. We call things Jesus that have nothing to do with Him. We use His name and birthday as an excuse for a massive consumer spending orgy every year - even though He NEVER said to celebrate His birthday and He wasn't even born in December! **GUILTY!**

Observe the Sabbath.

Where to even start? I don't even know how off track we are here, but Sunday better be more about GOD than FOOTBALL, I can tell you that! Can you legitimately say that all it takes to "observe the Sabbath" is an hour and fifteen minutes sitting in a pew? The Narrow Path can't possibly be THAT wide!! Are we sure it's not supposed to be on Saturday? Maybe every day. Whatever – we're still **GUILTY!**

Honor your father and mother.

This means respect them and their feelings but it also means that we are to bring them honor. We have converted our churches into institutions that displace and insult our elders. "Their music isn't loud enough. Their style isn't hip enough. Their faith isn't deep enough. Their God isn't cool enough. They need to get with the program and see that the wave of the future is bigger and louder and younger and with more feelings. If not, then we're going to have to leave them behind." We have NOT brought them honor and glory. We have prostituted or murdered the churches they built. We have lost traction on evangelism, missions, and every other emphasis that Jesus cares about. But we have churches so big that they need to meet in a stadium! **GUILTY!**

Do not murder.

What does this mean except that we kill someone so that we can gain something. Maybe it's not what we MEANT to do, but we still let them die so that we could have some advantage. Or worse yet, so we could have their stuff. At any given moment 200 MILLION Brothers and Sisters live on the very edge of starvation. Billions have died without Christ. But we have REALLY shiny new cars and churches that meet in stadiums. We sacrifice millions of souls every month to keep our comforts. It's not like we didn't know. We see starving children on TV and sponsor ONE for $30 - out of an average per capita income of tens of thousands - plus TRILLIONS of dollars of assets between us. We should know better than to think we're making a dent in the problem without some more sacrifice than that. We're intentionally letting them die to keep from having to share our stuff. **GUILTY!**

Do not commit adultery.

We cheat on the Bridegroom and our First Love through programs and fads and ecumenical movements that yoke us with those opposed to God. We have laid down with other religions, with the "world", with governments, with culture, with TV, with Hollywood, with Wall Street, with Sony Records, with political parties. We lay down with everything EXCEPT God! (Not to mention that 50% of clergy regularly use porn.) **GUILTY!**

Do not steal.

Each year the 'church' loses more to fraud and embezzlement to trusted people inside the organization ($16B – yeah, that's a "B" - as in BILLION) than it spends on foreign missions ($15B). We regularly try to get little old ladies to send their last dollar so we can buy a Bentley or a new plane or build a big building. And we tell them God is going to bless their blind faith in us. See #6 - if we're to share with each as they have need, then we HAVE to steal from the Brethren in other places in order to sustain our standard of living! **GUILTY!**

Do not lie.

Our denominations regularly falsify progress reports and spending projections. We spent BILLIONS on plans to reach the entire world with the gospel by the year 2000. We barely even kept up with population growth! No apologies, no explanations, just a renewed emphasis for more money. This doesn't even touch on all the snake oil salesmen pretending to be ministers of the Gospel that nobody seems to be willing to shut down and contend for the faith. Worst of all, we tell the world that this structure that we've built was Jesus' idea when it's really about our own egos and greed and selfishness. **GUILTY!**

Do not covet.

Did you read any of the ones above? We TEACH pastors to want bigger churches. We train MEN OF GOD to judge their effectiveness and worth on how many people want to come hear them speak. We TRAIN them in seminaries how to administrate effective building campaigns and fund growth. America is the ULTIMATE incarnation of coveting – and the 'church' is INDISTINGUISHABLE from culture. **GUILTY!**

We're not just doing this stuff a LITTLE BIT. We're talking about BILLIONS of people injured by this and TRILLIONS of dollars of assets being misdirected, wasted or stolen!! The lost potential in human souls in incalculable. Somebody is going to have to answer for this at the final judgement. NOW might be a really good time to weep and mourn before the altar. That's the formula for what to do when the locusts have eaten everything and the land is parched and dry. And I'm pretty sure that's about the state of the Church of America. All the good stuff has been sucked out. (Read the book of Joel.)

THE UNDENIABLE AXIOMS

According to Scripture, in the last days, apostasy (falling away) will be rampant in the Church.1 There will be false prophets, signs and wonders meant to deceive even the Elect. 2

It is our contention that God seeks to have systems built on HIS plan, not Man's. As regards AUTHORITY - His ways are not pyramid-shaped hierarchical systems following the will of a MAN at the top. If anything, it's a pyramid turned on it's head, with the leader being servant to all. As for authority, there is US and there is HIM. That's it. While there are delineations and delegations of responsibility, and there might be a chain of command to accomplish something, everyone in the chain should be looking to God for authority and submit as servant leaders to those around them. If we're walking in His Spirit, we worship no man.

God wanted Israel to worship and follow Him only. But they insisted on a King, so God gave them one knowing it would go badly - but that's what they wanted.3 They had it coming.

The Church has fallen into the same trap. Instead of worshiping God only, we've absorbed all the man-made models and adopted them as our own for centuries - millennia even! Go look at your church or denomination's organizational chart and see if it resembles the structures of Man and follows behind one person at the top. As for "Authority," in many cases we've usurped God's position and inserted ourselves at the top of the chain of command and insisted on obedience from the lower levels.

During the Millennial Reign of Christ, we will return to the perfect model.4 Christ as direct leader of all with no other steps or layers of authority in between. Even though others may reign with Him, it's inside His authority, not their own.5

God hates man-made organizational structures because they are innately sinful. He directed us to be respectful of those already in place.6 But He clearly instructed us to listen to HIM only, never to call another Father or Rabbi, when we were to be listening only to God.7

A lot of thought and prayer has gone into this. We've tried to explain the apostasy in the church and the dangers of the coming systems in the simplest possible terms. Based on scripture and clearly harmonious with the basic instincts of every person with a clear understanding of human nature. To deny this is to fly in the face of a basic understanding of human nature.

The Undeniable Axiom of Sinful Inertia

IF: You believe the Bible is the Word of God and is Truth;8

THEN: You believe that Man is a fallen, sinful creature and beyond redemption and perfection on his own.9

IF: You believe that Man is sinful (to whatever degree);10

THEN: You have to believe that the more Men in one organization, the more potential for sin comes with them. Like compounding interest. 11

IF: You want to have a positive impact on the World;12

THEN: You must acknowledge the sinful nature of Man and build structures to restrain or minimize it.13

IF: You base your structures on the ideas and management of Men;14

THEN: They are flawed and cannot restrain the mass of sin indefinitely.15

IF: The organization denies the sinful nature of Man;

THEN: It believes a lie, it builds no effective restraints and will immediately have a negative effect.

IF: The organization believes Man is sinful, except their own leaders;

THEN: It believes a lie, builds no restraints on the leaders and very quickly has a negative effect.

IF: The organization believes that ALL Men are sinful and builds restraints on ALL;

THEN: It operates in truth and can have a positive impact - to the limits of the restraints.

IF: The accumulation of sinful Men exceeds the limitations of the restraints;

THEN: The organization ceases to have positive impact and becomes something negative.

IF: You are Satan and you want to spit in the eye of God; 16

THEN: You build a One World Church that lies about the nature of man and has no real restraints on behavior.

Undeniable Axiom of Love of Money

IF: You believe the Bible is the Word of God and is Truth; 17

THEN: You believe the Bible when it says that the "Love of money is the root of all evil." 18

IF: You believe that the "Love of money is the root of all evil." 19

THEN: You have to recognize that it's not the money itself, but the LOVE of it. (Biblically speaking, anything that takes the place of God will do, but most often its money that's the issue.) 20

IF: You believe that money is a temptation when placed in the hands of sinful Man; 21

THEN: You have to believe that the bigger the pile of money, the greater the temptation.

IF: You have an organization that misunderstands the nature of Man and is already negative;

THEN: You have to see that if you give it LOTS of money, it will be VERY bad indeed.

IF: An organization believes ALL Men are sinful and builds restraints on ALL;

THEN: You can force it to and past the limits of it's restraints faster by just adding more money.

IF: An organization says it is positive but it's leader expresses a clear "Love of Money";

THEN: You can assume that organization has passed it's restraints and turned "Evil" and it is a lie. 22

IF: You are Satan and you want to spit in the eye of God; 23

THEN: You build a One World Government that controls ALL the money and has no restraints on the leaders. 24

The Undeniable Axiom of Synergy

IF: You want to prove the Bible to be True and right about the nature of Man;

THEN: You combine sinful Man and lots of money and watch to see what happens.

IF: You are Satan and you want to spit in the eye of God; 25

THEN: You build a One World Government and a One World Church, remove all restraints, thereby consolidating ALL of sinful Man into one mass and thus achieving "Maximum Possible Sinfulness." 26

IF: A Christian leader believes that the prophesied Millennial Reign of Christ is a time when Man will create a perfected, universal Christian church and Christian government on Earth to prepare the way for Christ to return;

THEN: That leader shows a flawed understanding of the nature of Man, has believed the Lie of Eve, and is (knowingly or unknowingly) playing right into the hands of the Enemy. Either way, you should RUN. And fast. 27

Basic Axiom Graph

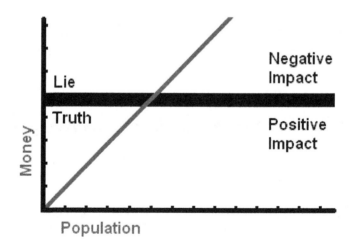

As Population goes up and Money goes up, sooner or later the Inertia of Sinfulness exceeds the restraints of the organization and it becomes something else entirely. It may still think it's positive, but it's not anymore. Government, church, business, family, individual - it doesn't matter, it's all sinful Man.

The reason it's hard for the "Rich" to enter the Kingdom 28 is because it all happens so much faster. The reason the poor churches of Smyrna and Philadelphia aren't chastised in Revelations Chapters 2 & 3 is because the "Rich" churches have already "jumped the shark" or crossed the line into being something other than their original nature. The poor churches are too worried about survival to have time to be in-fighting, debating new theology or getting lazy and soft.

What is this Truth and Lie stuff?

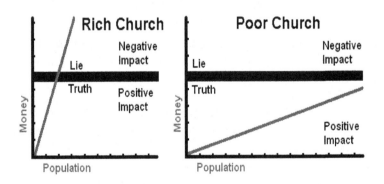

Let's say a church starts off as a small group of committed friends in an affluent community wanting to worship together and care for each other. They say, "We are a family. We care about each individual." Their numbers grow and with growth comes lots of cash. They build a building, they hire staff, they start new programs for outreach and care. They say, "We are a family. We care about each individual." At some point, if they're not VERY careful, they cross a line and their ACTIONS through their committees, their strategies, their staff decisions, their spending habits say, "We need more people here to pay the bills. We need to grow to justify the new gym. We need to be careful not to challenge or offend anyone, or we'll stop growing." But, they continue to SAY to themselves and to others, "We're a family. We care about each individual." But more and more people begin to feel that it's a lie. They sense the dissonance. Then leadership begins to "urge" people out of the church who disagree and wave a flag of warning. Then the pastor writes a best selling book about how he grew his church so big - so that other pastors can learn how to do it to their own churches. Then the pastor has lots of money AND lots of people to contend with - exactly the way Satan likes it. Even if they manage to resist the inertia of sinfulness until they are very large, there is constant need for watchfulness because a new leader (or a new heart in an old leader) can remove or diminish restraints very quickly.

Meanwhile, the poor church accumulated many times the number of members without ever changing their basic nature because they don't have enough assets to be covetous and contentious. They have just enough to care for each other and to worship God. No Christian coffeehouse, no amusement parks, no aerobics classes, no budget ministries, no best selling books, no giant egos. They say, "We are a family. We care about the individual." And while someday they might cross over the line, they can sustain it much longer because they are much more reliant on lay leaders and not paid staff and fancy programs and facilities. They have to be mobile and entrepreneurial. They don't have any resources to waste. Even so, there is need for watchfulness because a new leader (or a new heart in an old leader) can remove or diminish restraints very quickly.

This Axiom asserts that Mega churches with Mega assets are not Biblically what we should be striving for - and should always be treated with suspicion and much care. The burden of proof that they HAVE NOT crossed the line should constantly be on the pastor and lay leadership to verify to the people that in all things their actions and decisions match with their words. Steps should be taken to raise the restraints so that the threshold is higher - OR - steps should be taken to dramatically reduce the size of the organization and it's assets. One option would be to split into smaller units and divide up resources. Or to funnel money away from themselves as quickly as possible and get it directly to the most effective, Scripturally justifiable ministries.

What About Governments?

We should be wary of governments because everything is bigger and stronger and the mountains of money involved make it immediately highly dangerous. In addition, because government leadership can change quickly, the line between Truth and Lie is fluid and can flex up and down, taking you from a point of safety into a danger zone very quickly.

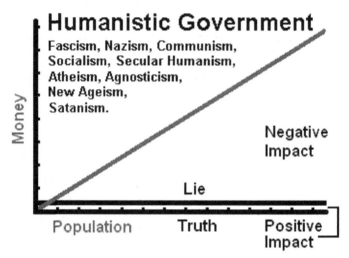

Humanistic Government

Fascism, Nazism, Communism,
Socialism, Secular Humanism,
Atheism, Agnosticism,
New Ageism,
Satanism.

Money

Negative
Impact

Lie

Population   Truth   Positive
Impact

Again, if any government or movement believes that they can create a Utopia on Earth if they'll just invent the correct structure, process, program, education, or worse, have the right single person in charge - they are GROSSLY misunderstanding the nature of Man and the lessons of history and are therefore highly dangerous.

If you give a government like that absolute authority and access to loads of cash, it will nearly immediately turn into a killing machine and eradicate any resistance to it's plan for "Peace". Because it has removed restraints on behavior since it believes Man to be inherently good - or even to have God within himself - whoever has the most power or charisma will call the shots and create whatever they want for themselves and crush any opposition.

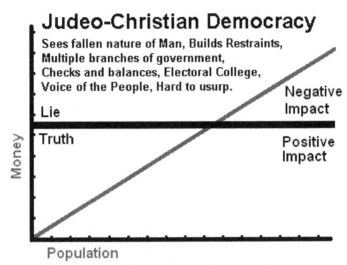

Judeo-Christian Democracy

**Sees fallen nature of Man, Builds Restraints,
Multiple branches of government,
Checks and balances, Electoral College,
Voice of the People, Hard to usurp.**

Negative
Impact

Lie

Truth

Positive
Impact

Money

Population

Conversely, if a government is founded from the very beginning on the idea that they are going to have to plan ahead to create complex ways to keep some powerful sinful Man (or Men) from exerting his will and taking over the whole government, it's possible that they could create a system that would hold off disaster for awhile.

Please don't take this to mean that this is what God wants! Far from it, these are all Man-made constructs that are inherently dangerous and innately un-Holy. Even the Judeo-Christian Democracy (or Representative Republic) has proven to work only by degrees and with lots of peaks and valleys along the way. It's nowhere near as linear as the over-simplified graph might suggest. It advocated slavery, welfare, racism, imperialism, manifest destiny and many others. (Many believe that American government has, for some time now, accumulated too much money and caused more harm than good. But that's not really our fight here.)

Again, the burden of proof should be squarely on Government to prove that it is still consistent with "We The People" and a concern for the rights of the citizenry. But, then, it's a flawed Man-made system and shouldn't be trusted anyway.

Conclusions

Between these Axioms you can chart the rise and fall of every government, every ministry, every man of God that fell, every future danger predicted in the Biblical prophecies. If an organization can identify that line before it gets to it, or feel it at the very early stages and act on it, there's a chance it can keep it's identity by addressing the issues quickly enough. Once an organization passes up and over that line, it will most likely result in painful division and much suffering. Or a long nasty lingering as it turns into something completely dangerous.

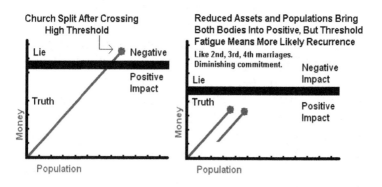

Here we see a church cross the threshold and it responds to the dissonance by splitting. Note that not all members are recovered. Some disappear, never to be seen again until the Day of Judgement, when we'll have to stand before God and accept responsibility for the kind of role models we were and take our punishment for the sheep that were lost while in our care. Both bodies from this split are now in even greater danger as they have begun a habit of dissension and division that will likely stunt the growth of their current efforts. Satan chuckles smugly.

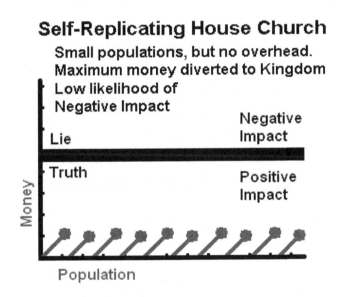

Self-Replicating House Church

Small populations, but no overhead.
Maximum money diverted to Kingdom
Low likelihood of
Negative Impact

Negative
Impact

Lie

Truth

Positive
Impact

Money

Population

One possible solution is the independent Self-Replicating House Church. These work because they simulate poverty. Or rather, they could be seen as the beginning stages of the Mega Church, but by their constant multiplication rather than consolidation, were never allowed to progress near the danger zone. Sort of like filling an ice cube tray where as each pocket fills it overflows and fills another. Bite sized ice chunks with their own compact lives and purpose - rather than one giant glacier with massive inertia. These are the model of the Chinese House Church movement. One other advantage is that they are very difficult to stomp out if persecution should begin. They can meet anywhere, be formed and reformed on demand and don't need formal leadership because many have been trained and can assume leadership. (This is also a model used effectively throughout history by many groups - with a wide varieties of motives. And has proven to be by far the most difficult to eliminate.)

Centrally Controlled Cell Church

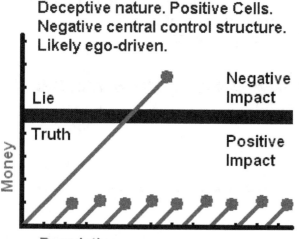

Deceptive nature. Positive Cells.
Negative central control structure.
Likely ego-driven.

Lie

Truth

Money

Negative
Impact

Positive
Impact

Population

One spin off that looks similar but isn't is the Centrally Controlled Cell Church. And example of this would be Paul Yonggi Cho's church where it looks like lots of independent cells, but they are really offshoots of a massive central church and are all VERY efficiently and tightly controlled and taxed. This is a difficult one because it's a great temptation for a big church to start cell groups as a way to multiply its reach without adding infrastructure. This should be seen as dangerous because they are not truly independent - not separate ice cubes capable of a life of their own. They are splinters off of the glacier and still owe their allegiance to it. They are tightly controlled specifically so that they WILL NOT spin off and become independent. That would diminish the power, money, and influence of the central control structure.

Are you getting it? This isn't necessarily about just the macro view. It applies down to families, teams, classrooms.

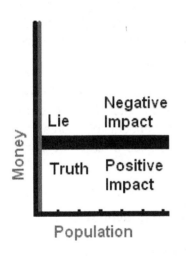

You see, big populations aren't required, the Axiom works even with the individual. Say a person writes a best selling book, wins the lottery, inherits big money, finds a copy of the Declaration of Independence in their attic, records a hit record, whatever.

If they don't accurately assess the dangers of their own nature, put systems in place to constrain and restrain the temptations and channel the blessing to do God's work, the dangers to themselves and others from having a massive windfall are enormous. The lie begins with, "I've waited a long time for this.

Spending it on me won't hurt anybody. I earned it by picking the right Lotto numbers." And as groupies and salesmen start to accumulate, it quickly becomes, "They love me! I must be a great guy! I deserve this! God must want me to have that new Ferrari." Before you know it, it's "I'm indestructible! I'm practically a god." Then, late one night at a strip bar it becomes, "I AM God! I can do anything!" Then they die tragically when their Ferrari shoots off the highway because they dropped their mirror and took their eyes off the road.

Of course, it doesn't always happen like that. Sometimes they live long happy lives full of reward and enjoyment, completely full and content in themselves, wanting for nothing. God says to enjoy it because that's all the reward there is. Then they die and get to report to Jesus what they did with all the blessings they were given.

Either way, you can see why Jesus suggested that it was EXTREMELY difficult for the rich to enter the kingdom of heaven. There is a massive amount of inertia and temptation to overcome when big piles of cash are laying around.

Think you can deny the undeniable?

Let's hear it.

I wrote this in 2004 and NOBODY has even TRIED to show me where it's wrong.

Fotm@FellowshipOfTheMartyrs.com

"Axiom" :

1 : a maxim widely accepted on its intrinsic merit

2 : a statement accepted as true as the basis for argument or inference

3 : an established rule or principle or a self-evident truth

(Websters New World Dictionary)

"Undeniable Axioms" References

1. 2 Thess. 2:3	15. Rom. 7:8-11
2. Matthew 24:24	16. Isaiah 50:6
3. 1 Samuel 9:20	17. John 17:17
4. Rev. 20:1-6	18. 1 Tim. 6:10
5. Rev. 20:4,6	19. Col. 3:1-2
6. Heb. 13:17	20. Mat 26:14-16
7. Matthew 23:9	21. Acts 5:1-11
8. Psa. 119:160	22. Rev. 3:17-18
9. Romans 3:23	23. Isaiah 50:6
10. Romans 8:3	24. Rev. 13:25, Isaiah 50:6
11. Romans 7:13	26. Rev. 13:16-17; 17:1-6
12. Matt 5:13, Isaiah 58	27. Matt. 24:16
13. Rom. 8:12-14	28. Matt. 19:24
14. Gal. 1:10-12	

WHO ARE THE PHARISEES?

You know the Seven Woes that Jesus calls down on the Pharisees in Matthew 23? It's clear he doesn't think much of them as a group. They were showy and extravagant, they loved the places of honor and the feeling that they knew more than anyone else, they would work hard to make a new convert and then corrupt them into their own twisted image, they put their faith in the material rather than the spiritual, they gave money instead of giving of their mercy and time and faithfulness, they were full of greed and self-indulgence, they looked shiny and new on the outside but were hollow on the inside.

Did you ever know someone like that? Have you seen religious leaders act that way? I'm sure we all have someone that we could point to and say meets at least some of the characteristics Jesus ascribed to the Pharisees. Have you known people like the Rich Young Ruler that loved God but couldn't take that final step of obedience?

Through my own experiences growing up overseas as a missionary kid and as we continue to grow our new missions organization, AcrossCountries.com *{now on hold until we get*

Liberty fixed} we've had a great opportunity to get a little glimpse of how Christians in America are viewed from the outside.

A really terrible thought has been gnawing at me lately. In our local circle of influence we can usually point to someone that we can describe as a "Pharisee." But if you gathered the Christians from all over the world and asked them to point out who was most like the Pharisees Jesus described – WE'RE the ones at whom they would all be pointing!

Over 95% of available Christian resources are being spent in the West. Half of the world has never seen even a single page of the Bible! When we send missionaries over there and convert someone, the first thing we do is impose our denominational distinctives and enmesh them in our theological squabblings over issues that aren't central to the faith.

There are Christian Brothers and Sisters starving to death and still being faithful, finding a way to give even in poverty. Their commitment and joy in the Lord is awesome and should shame all of us. They go and preach in the most dangerous places, knowing they could be killed (and frequently are) - while we are unwilling to talk to our neighbors for fear of looking like a "Jesus freak."

Previously I've mentioned that the United States gross domestic product (GDP) is about $10 Trillion per year. Regular church-going Christians control as much as $3 Trillion per year of that through our personal income (roughly equivalent to the ENTIRE annual spending of the U.S. Government). We control many, MANY times that when you calculate the value of our stocks, savings, real estate, life insurance, businesses and other assets. What are we accomplishing with it? From the perspective of Christians in other countries, we're just gorging ourselves while others stand and wait to be fed – both physically and spiritually.

I can't find any Biblical justification for some Christians having assets worth tens of trillions of dollars while other Christians (on an income of $1 or $2 per day) survive and build churches and minister to others around them. In fact, it seems to me there are some very specific scriptures to which we should probably pay more attention. For example:

> **1 Timothy 6:17-19** (NIV) - "Command those who are rich in this present world not to be arrogant nor to put their hope in wealth, which is so uncertain, but to put their hope in God, who richly provides us with everything for our enjoyment. Command them to do good, to be rich in good deeds, and to be generous and willing to share. In this way they will lay up treasure for themselves as a firm foundation for the coming age, so that they may take hold of the life that is truly life."

Or maybe Mark 10:23; "Jesus looked around and said to his disciples, "How hard it is for the rich to enter the kingdom of God!" (See also: I Timothy 6:8-10, Luke 16, Mark 12:41-44)

You think you're not rich? Compared to what? Compared to your boss or the guy in that giant house down the street or someone on TV? You think Jesus is talking about someone else? I've got news for you, in today's world, He is talking about YOU – and me. Half the people in the world don't sleep on a bed! Half the world earns $3 a day or less!

And if He's talking about churches, it's OUR churches that will have the hardest time at the final Judgement, not those in India or China or Ethiopia. The VAST percentage of all Christian resources are in the Western countries. In our bank accounts and those of our churches. Two BILLION people live their life undernourished. 700 million live in slums.

I'm not telling you what to do with your wealth. I just ask that you will pray and ask God to guide you. If you decide you want to make a commitment to help, feel free to contact us or at least read more about what is happening out there.

GOD – THE SUPREME BANKER

I've been thinking a lot about this. Because I'm a business guy, I think in financial terms. See if this makes any sense to you.

When we're born God opens two bank accounts for us. One is a checking account and the other is a retirement account. As soon as we are old enough to know better, our sin immediately begins to overdraw the checking account. We might do good works and care for the sick, orphans, widows, etc. - and we DO get credit for that, but it gets locked into the retirement account. The checking account is unaffected. NOTHING, nothing, nothing can redeem us of our indebtedness and overdrawn status on our checking account - except the blood of Jesus. We are bankrupt and condemned because of the checking account. The retirement account can't be used to pay our debt.

When we accept Christ and lay our lives at the feet of the Cross, He instantly brings us back up to zero. We are debtfree! Praise God! We're redeemed. But ... mostly we are too stupid and stubborn and sinful to be able to stay at zero. Before long we start sinning and our debt accumulates again. Now, we might be doing good works throughout and tithing and feeding the poor and maybe even doing great miracles and preaching our hearts out - but all that does is store up in our retirement account. Sooner or later, we realize our indebtedness again and repent and Jesus zeroes out the checking debt again. Holiness is living at zero. There is no positive balance possible in the checking account. We can't exceed holiness - the best we can hope for in this life is a lack of sinfulness (debt) that keeps us at zero.

Only those who are debt-free in their checking account will be counted as worthy - and ONLY THEN can they cash in their retirement accounts. There will be many on that day that say "Lord, Lord, look at my giant retirement account!" and He will say, "Yep, but that wasn't the main point. Get your goatishness out of here." (Or something like that.) MANY will have done good works that they will never be able to cash in. Or they did some, but for the wrong motives. (See Matt. 25)

For me it's really simple. Try to stay at zero (holiness/purity) and repent ALL the time, just in case. Then, if I have ONE hour of my time to spend, do I rack up more treasure in heaven watching TV or visiting someone in prison or feeding the homeless? If I have just ONE dollar to give, do I get more treasure in heaven for helping buy a chandelier for the sanctuary or feeding an orphan in Ghana? And if I help a servant of God and thereby get a share of HIS reward, then who is the hottest stock around and how can I get in on it? (Matt. 10:40-42) That is, who has the biggest pile of treasure and how can I help them get more? Is it my megachurch pastor, the televangelist with a new book out, the missionaries from denominational headquarters or the barefoot native pastor in India that has planted 100 thriving churches among the most unreached and lives on $1 a day?

I'm not saying you financially "flagellate" yourself and live on nothing. I'm saying EVERY dollar is God's - so you ask Him, "Lord, can I buy an ice cream cone with this dollar? Lord, should I feed an orphan with this dollar? Lord, should I help buy a million dollar chandelier for the sanctuary?" Sometimes He says it's OK for me to have ice cream, or a newer car, or whatever. He cares for His own, He doesn't want me to starve. But He always wants His money spent according to HIS priorities. If you'll listen and then be obedient, even if it's hard, it's likely He'll decide you can be trusted with more and more money. We're to be good stewards, not just to hand it over to any schmo with a 501(c)(3) without asking any questions.

Oh ... and if you think I'm arguing against a "once saved, always saved" view of salvation, I'm really not. I honestly don't know if a sincere prayer at church camp when you were eight is enough to get you in the door or not. But I know Jesus expects a lot more out of us than just having once said a prayer and then done whatever we wanted the rest of the time. It just seems like the Narrow Path HAS to be more narrow than that! He says that if we love Him, we'll OBEY Him. Lots of people are going to call Him "Lord" on that day and but still won't make the cut. (Matt. 25:41-46)

I'm just pointing out that just because you might have done some good stuff, doesn't necessarily mean you'll get to cash in on that reward if you're not seeking holiness. You'll have to seek God and see if He says you're where you need to be with Him. That's between you two. But it's kind of important that you'd get this sorted out as soon as possible.

EMAIL FROM RENEE IN RESPONSE TO THE APOLOGY TO THE WORLD LETTER

Dear brother,

I've been hungering for more of God all my life. I've been to just about every denomination there is. I've sang in the choir, taught Sunday school, led folks to the Lord, memorized Scriptures, was Praise and Worship leader, Pastored a Church, on and on and on. And I've always been haunted by a HUGE HUNGER for more of our Adored. I'm a simple woman. I'm not smart or even cute. I'm of no importance whatsoever. I've been sick all my life (48 years old) and for the last 12 years I've been housebound with really bad health. I've watched myself become "hedged in" like Job, by the hand of our Loving Father. Cut off from family and friends, no health, no anything. I haven't been to church in many years because I couldn't take it anymore.

When one is suffering, and in pain with health problems, and with a broken heart because of one's own "flesh" (the old nature that doesn't wanna take up the Cross) AND with a grieving spirit because one wants MORE OF GOD, and one is weeping over lost loved ones............well, let me just say that I didn't fit in with any churches around here. My hubby is saved so there are two of us who fellowship together.

Anyway, even though I feel like I've been following in Job's footsteps, I believe with all my heart that our Adored is going to MOVE once again on behalf of His Own who are crying out to Him like the widow of Luke 18. ALL MY LIFE I'VE BEEN PLAGUED WITH A HUNGER FOR MORE OF GOD! Yes, I use the word plague because it seems so "wrong" when compared to the partying church of today. I've had this incredible hunger all my life, and used to weep by the hour when I'd read of Believers in the Bible.......OH to love God the way HE DESERVES TO BE LOVED. But brother, I KNEW my Flesh well, and without the Grace of God I could never love Him or anyone else. I'm a crusty old crow, and my flesh does NOT like taking up my daily cross, sigh.

Then, I stumbled onto a book about Saints of old like George Fox, Charles G. Finney, Smith Wigglesworth, etc, and I wept for days and days, and I've never been able to get rid of a DESIRE for more of God. I'll admit, may God forgive me, that in years gone by I did try to ignore it, and play church like others advised me to do. But it just wasn't me. The old hymn says "Just as I am" and I'm too stupid to be anything less than myself, for better or for worse. Besides, our Tender Eternal knows all about me anyway, so why try to hide anything from Him?!!

Brother, did you read how Mary was LOOKING FOR HER LORD outside of the tomb on the day He arose? Just imagine the scene.......Heaven is jam-packed with excitement! After 33 years, the One Who "used" to sit at the Right Hand of the Father will be coming back HOME. Every flower in glory must have been blooming with EXTRA joy that day! And then......the Father Speaks, and the Holy Spirit RAISES HIM FROM THE DEAD!!!! OH GLORY HE'S COMING UP.....HE'S COMING UP HERE ONCE AGAIN, RAISED VICTORIOUS!!!!! Oh the excitement, and joy!!!! But wait.......what is going on? Where IS HE? Why hasn't He come yet? What is the hold up? WHAT ON EARTH IS GOING ON? I'll tell you what ON EARTH is going on........the simple, yet DEEP LOVE OF A WOMAN FOR HER ADORED STOPPED THE LORD JESUS DEAD IN HIS TRACKS!! Huh? That's right! You see, the angels spoke to her when she looked into the tomb, but instead of hurrying home to her Women's Bible study group to bask in the glory of telling her "story" of seeing an angel, see just turned away from the grave and continued looking for HIM! SHE ONLY HAD EYES FOR HIM! Her heart was breaking. She was so heartbroken that she couldn't think of anything else. How on earth was she going to get through this day? WHERE WAS HE? Wherever He was, she HAD to find Him, HAD TO BE WITH HIM.

At this time our Blessed Redeemer is on His way HOME, but STOPS SHORT OF THE FATHER!!!!!!!! ABSOLUTELY INCREDIBLE!!!!!!!! What manner of LOVE IS THIS, that the Father (anxious to SEE His victorious SON) graciously steps aside to a lowly woman's desires? WHY? BECAUSE HE RECOGNIZES THE DEMAND OF HER BROKEN HEART, and gives way to the LOVE HE HIMSELF PUT THERE! OH WHAT A GOD!!!! The heart has its reasons whereof reason knows nothing. Not a Bible verse, but so incredible TRUE.

So, she sees the Gardener, and says to Him.........where have you taken Him to? She offers to take Him away even though she (being a lady) may have had a hard time taking a dead body anywhere. But you know what? She LOVED HIM so much that she didn't even think about that. All she wanted was TO BE WITH HIM. So, her heart drove her to ignore the angels, and LOOK for Him. So, she is forced (compelled by love) to question the Gardener. And then......PRAISE GOD......OUR ADORED REVEALS HIMSELF TO HER!!!!! LOVE ANSWERS LOVE! She was the FIRST to SEE HIM raised from the dead! And she reaches out to Him, but He says no because He hasn't yet been to the Father. So, LOVE FORCED LOVE TO STOP THAT DAY on the way Home to Glory, and comfort the hurting pains of a broken heart before going on HOME to the Father. And Mary became the first one to spread the GOOD NEWS that our Adored IS RISEN!!!

Dear brother, I'm jealous of her. I'm jealous of King David. I tell you that I want to love God SO MUCH that the Angels in Heaven BLUSH!!! I want to LOVE HIM like HE has NEVER been loved before, and Christ IN ME is able to do it. But my fleshy nature needs the Power of the Holy Spirit from on High to flow through me to do so. I've never been Baptised in the Holy Spirit. I've been through some bad experiences concerning that, and now am waiting for the Lord to pour out His REAL Holy Spirit. I want to be so filled with the LORD JESUS that my flesh is too danged scared to even try to come out, lol. I want to be so filled with His HOLY OIL that I leave marks on the floor as I walk. Well, okay, I don't expect to leave actual marks, but brother, DO YOU KNOW

WHAT I MEAN? I'm no good to anyone the way I am. I need the LORD in ALL HIS FULNESS. Call it revival, call it a new song, call it whatever you want to call it. All I know is that I feel like Patrick Henry: Give me LIBERTY (where the Spirit of the Lord is, there is Liberty) OR GIVE ME DEATH (to die is gain). If Mr. Henry could feel that way about real estate, then how much more the Church about THE LIVING GOD?!! I'm tired of myself the way I am, and tired of watching sinners suffering, and living without the Lord. WHERE IS MORE OF THE LORD? I feel like even after 12 eternities I'm going to be wanting MORE of Him. Please pray for me dear brother. My hubby has caught this desire now, and we both felt alone in this until we heard about you from another brother we just heard of a few days ago. We live in St. Louis County. So, we are also SHOW ME JESUS Saints, heehee.

Well, brother, I'm sorry for going on and on, but praise God, as tears flow, I've got to tell you that I've been so lonely, not knowing that others were hungering for more of our Adored also. Praise God for His mercy. I'm in a lot of pain or my hubby and I would come to that John the Baptist conference. Please pray for us. We need more of the Lord.

God bless you dear brother, and thank you. I was going to post at that discussion forum, but it is so new, and I felt like I'd be spoiling it. I feel all thumbs when saying stuff over the net. Heck, I feel like I'm all thumbs anyway. I'm sure I'm the one who gave our Lord Jesus all that white hair that He has now according to the description of Him in Revelation, lol.

love to you from your sis, Renee'

A little child shall lead them... :-)

DOUG'S PERSONAL EXPERIENCE WITH THE HOLY SPIRIT

(Written Jan. 25, 2005 – edited March, 18, 2007)

I had been praying and aching for several months to see the Holy Spirit come in power and do something. I had read Acts over and over and we were having a Bible Study time on Sunday nights at my shop with the folks I respected the most. What I was really hoping for was that book of Acts, Pentecost, tongues of fire stuff – but had no idea what I was doing. TWICE in my life (before November of 2004) had I ever even been in a room with someone speaking in tongues - and one of those was at a concert with like 2500 other people. They didn't teach me anything about this in the Baptist church except to be skeptical and suspect it's made up - or worse, that it's from the enemy. (Even now, I'm still hyper-sensitive to it and it's appropriate use. Which is a good thing.)

Round about November, Andrew (Strom) and I met and had lunch and he liked a lot of what I had been saying about the problems in the church. He asked me if I had been baptized in the Holy Spirit and I said, "Huh?" We talked about it for awhile and he encouraged me to read up and pray on it. A couple days later I went down to his Sunday evening meeting he was having and he asked if I would like to speak - which of course I did. Had a good impact, although kind of preaching to the choir since his crowd is already sort of outside of the standard "church" streams. But that was also the first night the Schafers were there and we really hit it off.

The following Tuesday (11/23/04), Andrew was having a prayer meeting at the home of one of the folks in his group and suggested I come and they would pray for me to receive "the Blessing" - that is, to be filled with the Holy Spirit. They were all his family and a few other folks he trusted a lot. (I've learned not to let just ANYBODY lay hands on me!) I was fully primed by the time it rolled around. We had a meal and talked for awhile and then we prayed a little and then they were going to pray on me. They wanted me to sit in a chair in the middle of the room and I said, "Heck, no! I'm kneeling. No way I'm going to sit there all comfy before God." So, about four or five of them are praying on me in tongues pretty loud. It was hard to concentrate, but I just decided that they were nice folks, so I didn't care how they wanted to pray as long as they were sincere and they helped me get what I came for.

Since I was a kid, I never prayed for anything but wisdom. It's just a math problem to me. Solomon was the smartest guy ever, that's what Solomon prayed for, that must make it the wisest thing to ask for. It's always at the top of the list of

Gifts in I Corinthians and elsewhere. Why pray for tongues? It's at the bottom of the list! Just my business instinct, I guess. Go for the good stuff.

Anyway, so they prayed on me for about 30-40 minutes (I think) as I begged for the Holy Spirit and promised to do right if He would bless me. I promised God that if He would empower me, I was willing to give up anything and endure anything. I just wanted to be the most dangerous person on the planet to the cause of evil. I wanted to sniff it out and rip out it's heart with my teeth. I wanted to be God's pit bull. I wanted wisdom, I wanted a high vantage point, to see through the eyes of Jesus. To know what people needed to hear to convict them, to burn away all the impurities and see just the pure kernel of the essence of what we should be doing to please Him.

I begged Him to shine a light on anything in my heart that was in the way and I would scrub it out. Together, He and I just went through one thing after another. I have plenty of sins - maybe not big ones as the world judges them – but there is plenty of darkness in my heart for which to repent. I had to drop some angers at old bosses or girl friends or others. At one point, He said, "You're pretty good with the orphans, but you're lacking with the widows since you haven't gone to see your grandmother in the hospital." So I promised on the spot that I would go see her before the week was up and make it all right. That seemed to satisfy him. I kept getting a warm fuzzy feeling like this was my time and He was going to answer my prayers, but then it stalled out. About then, I think Andrew and them were getting tired (they have to lean over, because I refused the chair!) and he asks me if there is anything in the way or if there is a history of Masonry in my family. I said, "No," and we just all agreed to pray that the Lord would shine a light on what was the problem. Nearly as soon as we started praying again, the Holy Spirit reminded me that there wasn't any Masonry, but I had been in a fraternity in college that required that you take an oath of secrecy on God. Even though when I was an initiate I hadn't said the oath at the time, later on I was the ritualist and administered it to others. I instantly repented of it and renounced it and stepped away from that. That was the last thing in the way.

Just then, Andrew suggested that maybe I should stand up. When I did, the vision started. I prayed for wisdom and to see through the eyes of Jesus. To me that's just a higher vantage point - where you can see more of the Big Picture. Both the love and the anger, the judgement and the mercy. I had prayed to take on any task, no matter the cost. So what He showed me was as much wisdom and responsibility as I could handle without passing out. I distinctly remember a sense from Him that I didn't really know how big a thing I had asked for, but He was going to show me as much as I could handle anyway. He was glad that I asked, but almost grinning because He knew what it would do to me! Fatherly love like when your nine year old son wants to build his own race car or something.

So for about ten minutes or so (maybe more), God ran this through my head. It was as if I was in outer space looking down on the globe. On the right side is a reel of faces going by. All children, all different colors. The vast majority are crying or hurting or sick or dying. It was like fast forwarding a DVD, they whip by real fast and then it stops long enough to see a few, then they whip along again. On the left side of the globe is the outline of America and a nasty, inky blackness covering it with tendrils spreading out all over the world. I knew that this was the sin of the church - selfishness, apostasy, greed, pride, waste, denominationalism, fraud, prosperity gospel, etc. that was spreading out from America and reaching all over the world. The reel of pictures of kids was running full speed. The Lord said, "You wanted to see through my eyes, I'm going to show you ALL of it." He knows that I have a heart for kids (as He does) and that's the way He sees us anyway, so that's how He showed it to me - as innocents hurt, killed, maimed, abused, impoverished, starving because of the nasty blackness coming out of America. It was clear to me that these weren't little kids, these were God's children of all ages. And He made it clear I was seeing ALL of them. I mean ALL of them. I honestly believe that all six billion plus spun by. Maybe more, maybe it was all of them EVER. I can't even comprehend it. But He made it clear that they were dying because of US and what WE have done maliciously or selfishly neglected to do to push back the darkness. I had a horrible pain in my chest and ached and groaned instantly.

Andrew's middle girl, Kirsten (who was about 11), was praying hard on my right and without really knowing I'd done it, I grabbed ahold of her and hugged her to me and just stroked her head and cried big huge sobs. Out loud I kept begging God to stay His judgement and apologizing for what we'd done to the children. I just felt so much pain in my chest and I was groaning and crying and just kept watching and saying out loud, "Oh, the children! What we've done to the children! Please help us save them, Lord. I'm SO sorry." (Or some derivative or combination thereof.) And I REALLY, REALLY needed Kirsten at that moment as a real live kid I could pet and hug and cry over. (She and I are bonded in a way I can't really explain. She just let me pet her head and drip on her and kept right on praying for me. What a good sport!) This went on for a long time (to me) and then finally faded with Him saying, "YOU'RE responsible for them. You said you would, so now it's on YOU." I asked the Lord, "What do you mean?!" He said, "You wanted to be the most dangerous person on the planet, you wanted to see through the eyes of Jesus, I showed you everybody, now you're responsible." I said, "Lord, you're telling lots of other people they're responsible, too, right? It's not just me?" He said, "It doesn't matter, you said you were willing, so now GO!" I got it then (and still do) that somehow I personally have a responsibility to reach them all with the Gospel and turn this thing around. (Still trying to figure out how that's fair -- or possible!)

After it was over, I was still in a lot of pain in my chest. We sat back in the circle and I was groaning and wincing in pain. They asked me what I had seen and I tried to tell them, but it was hard to breathe and every time I'd close my eyes I'd get a glimpse of it again and it would hurt. Like an ice pick in my chest. The folks there wanted to reassure me that it was OK that I hadn't spoken in tongues - which I found myself HIGHLY irritated about since that's not why I was there. I said, "Hey. I got what I came for and then some! I will never be the same. I asked for wisdom and to see the big picture and that's what I got." There was a kind of quiet pressure that the tongues part was REALLY important, but they could see clearly that something big had happened and I was still sitting there wincing and groaning and twitching in pain every so often. Mostly I was too distracted processing it to have been bothered, but it was an important lesson about the subconscious pressure that can be put on the experience without even realizing it. They all seemed to NEED tongues to happen at that moment, but then every single one of them went around and told about how when they started speaking in tongues it was some time after their Baptism with the Holy Spirit, some of them a LOT later. I didn't comment much at the time, but I thought it interesting that they all felt it SHOULD happen a certain way, but none of THEM had it happen to them that way. I didn't particularly want tongues, so it didn't much matter. At last Andrew made the most sense when he explained it mathematically (without meaning to). He explained that tongues is a way to let the Spirit help relieve you of a burden so heavy that words won't work anymore and that I would probably need it sooner or later if the pressure was high. THAT made sense, because I knew what I was carrying! So at that point, I started to see that it was coming and I was going to need it. (A couple days later I had to get a physical for the adoption anyway, so because of the chest pain I had them run cholesterol checks, just be sure I wasn't having a heart attack! But I checked out perfect!)

Anyway, we said goodbye and I got in my van to drive home, still wincing from the pain and moaning and groaning with the weight of what I'd seen. For several days, every time I closed my eyes I would see it again and wince and ache and moan. For a couple of days after, I had this amazing love for everybody. I would go about my day just wanting to hug on people and pinch their cheeks because I just KNEW how much Jesus loved them! I knew they were one of the children that had whipped by in my vision. I went into Wal-Mart and everyone was SOOO beautiful! But that faded in a couple of days - especially in Wal-Mart.

Things started to change instantly. I can't play video games anymore. I can't watch TV. I can't curse. I can't survive without at least a couple of hours of praying a day. The

Bible is opened up for me and I see things and connections that I've never heard ANYBODY say before. Lately, I can't go anywhere without my Bible and I spend every extra minute in it. Sin repulses me. I've surely spoken out of turn or pridefully or not considered someone's feelings or misprioritized my time or been irritated - but am instantly aware of it and repentant. I have a hard time getting any work done because I want to talk about God all the time - to anybody - and when I do, they are convicted. I get physically pained if a dirty spam email pops up before I can delete it. I can't even think about anything intimate with anyone other than my wife. Can't even consider it or picture it. Gone is the fighting at home over stupid stuff, lots more love all the time even though it's a hard walk and there's still disagreement. One night He woke me up at 2am and said to pray for my wife. Comfy in bed with her on my arm, warm blankets, eyes closed - I prayed until 6:30am without a break or dozing off or anything. Just like on auto-pilot, but not asleep. Which is nuts cause I'll fall asleep typing sometimes and bash my head on the keyboard. Much less, comfy in bed with my eyes closed! Plus I'm fasting now. Never know when or for how long, but I shouldn't be able to fast even a half a day with my hypoglycemia. Now I get up in the morning and go to the fridge and ask the Lord if I get to eat today. Sometimes He says yes and sometimes no. If I can physically GET the food in my mouth, I'm not fasting. It's not even a decision anymore. In the last two months He has had me fasting several times for 24 hours or less, once for almost three days and once for almost four days. Just water. No cravings, no pain, no headaches or dizziness or weakness. Usually ends with some big event for which I need to be fully concentrated or clean. Then I can get food in my mouth again. I actually look forward to fasting because I know I'm being obedient and I know it's going to end with something that will glorify Him. (Once was the Christmas day trip to the children's hospital.) Plus it's evidence of a supernatural protection over me, because I should NOT medically be able to fast at all. *{Update: Since this was written the fasting changed to mostly without even water, 1-8 days at a time, on average 3 or 4 days a week without water for over two years. That's just God! I lost over 70 pounds and feel great!}*

The following three weeks (after 11/23) held a constant conversational closeness with the Holy Spirit and some AMAZING prayer time where He laid out more of what is coming and made promises to me of weapons I would have in order to fight the battles ahead (including the gift of healing and discernment/deliverance of evil spirits and other stuff). In that time I got to participate in two good friends getting full of the Spirit - one dear friend at another of Andrew's meetings (who started singing in tongues right on the spot!) and one by myself in the office with her. Also gave some really hard specific prophetic words individually to specific people that changed them. Also in that time, the Schafers came to work with us. (James and Cindy have been such a critical component of the learning that has been crammed into those first 12 weeks! I can't even begin to imagine what I would have done without their intercession and gentle advice and example.) God sent this missionary family from Canada to Liberty, Missouri to spend their time at my for-profit furniture store and help grow me!

Nonetheless, the following three weeks were miserable because I felt a growing despair and unhappiness and darkness. I was getting a massive pressure inside and no release valve. I was praying desperately for the gift of tongues at that point because I felt I couldn't get it all out. The burden on me felt huge and I wasn't getting any relief. Then bad things started happening at home - the sewer backs up into the basement and the dog throws up all over and the kid is acting up and the wife is sick. Lots of people are heavily burdened and are praying for me like crazy. My wife didn't know what to do with me, because she was very skeptical of the "charismatic thing" and I'm up at all hours and crying and praying and moaning and groaning. She said, "Where's your joy? We know who wins in the end! Why all the crying?" But I can't help but see the badness.

One Sunday evening, I'm sitting in the living room asking what to do and the Lord tells me to read Hosea. So I'm reading Hosea with a towel over my head (just needed to get UNDER something!) and crying and shaking and rocking back and forth as the Lord shows me how desperately bad the judgement on America will be because we're doing everything in Hosea that brought judgement on Israel, except with thousands of times worse. Then Rachael wakes up from her nap and walks through the living room, shakes her head at me and says, "Except for the nonsense syllables, you might as well be speaking in tongues for the way you sound." Well, she often has bursts of wisdom hidden in the most unlikely, sarcastic comments, so something clicked in me that it was so weird that she would say that since I'd been praying so hard about tongues.

So the Lord kind of nudged me that I ought to figure out what it was I was doing and led me through some "moaning and groaning" scriptures. Romans 8:26 is probably the most well-known: *26 In the same way, the Spirit helps us in our weakness. We do not know what we ought to pray for, but the Spirit himself intercedes for us with groans that words* cannot express. *27 And he who searches our hearts knows the mind of the Spirit, because the Spirit intercedes for the saints in accordance with God's will.*

Others include:

Romans 8:23 (all NIV) - *Not only so, but we ourselves, who have the firstfruits of the Spirit, groan inwardly as we wait eagerly for our adoption as sons, the redemption of our bodies.*

2 Corinthians 5:2 - *Meanwhile we groan, longing to be clothed with our heavenly dwelling,*

2 Corinthians 5:4 - *For while we are in this tent, we groan and are burdened, because we do not wish to be unclothed but to be clothed with our heavenly dwelling, so that what is mortal may be swallowed up by life.*

Isaiah 59:11 - *We all growl like bears; we moan mournfully like doves. We look for justice, but find none; for deliverance, but it is far away.*

Micah 1:8 - *Because of this I will weep and wail; I will go about barefoot and naked. I will howl like a jackal and moan like an owl. 9 For her wound is incurable; it has come to Judah. It has reached the very gate of my people, even to Jerusalem itself.*

But (unfortunately) the ONE that most resonates with me is :

Ezekiel 21:6 - *6 "Therefore groan, son of man! Groan before them with broken heart and bitter grief. 7 And* *when they ask you, 'Why are you groaning?' you shall say, 'Because of the news that is coming. Every heart will melt and every hand go limp; every spirit will become faint and every knee become as weak as water.' It is coming! It will surely take place, declares the sovereign LORD ." The word of the LORD came to me: "Son of man, prophesy and say, 'This is what the Lord says: " 'A sword, a sword, sharpened and polished- sharpened for the slaughter, polished to flash like lightning!"* (... And other scariness following!)

The next day, I talked to Janice and James and Andrew about it and whether that's what maybe I could have in the slot where tongues would normally be - 'cause I'd been doing it since that same night (11/23), even during the vision, but nobody thought to tell me to consider that that was one of the options! So that Monday I just went around the office wheezing and groaning and the pressure went down. That night I got home and confirmed it with God in prayer time (3 times) and He told me to stop asking for something else, that this is what I was to have and it was better for me anyway (and explained why). Glory to God!!

From then on I've been moaning and groaning and grumbling and wheezing all the time to get the pressure down. This gift was given to me this way for specific personal reasons and is very powerful. I feel like I could move mountains with it. I was talking to David Kirkwood about it and He asked if I'd read anything about it because it's a consistent component in all the major revival movements and some folks try to fake it. I hadn't and haven't since. If I had known it was one of the options, I would not have prayed desperately for tongues for three weeks! So he had to rethink his sense of the validity of it as reality and not myth - since I have it and didn't even know what it was. I think it's cool because it's not exactly subject to the I Corinthians 14 rules for tongues. In fact, God actually orders Ezekiel to do it in public! Also, I can do it all the time and most folks don't notice - or just think I have asthma. Also, it's very breathing focused and I asked Him about why this and He said, "To keep you from being prideful because every breath is MINE and if you don't use it to MY glory, I might decide you don't need any more breaths." Zowie! That got my attention! He also said that, "The time is coming when you will be an object lesson. People won't have time to waste anymore as things move faster. They will have between THIS breath and the next one to decide if they are going to dedicate that next breath (and all after it) to me. If they don't, they could be lost forever or like Ananias and Sapphira who held back and lied to Me, so I just made them stop breathing. Someday people will only have between this HEARTBEAT and the next one to decide who's team they are on and get right!" Things are moving faster all the time.

During the last 12 weeks, I have been through four or five major philosophical directional frameworks, tested and rejected bunches of theories and ideas, started two or three new websites, tempered my anger at the church and now refocusing and finally finding the pure central kernel of what God wants. Just now finding a voice that He can live with and God can use without creating more trouble for myself by distracting from Him. The LAST thing I want to do is say something that will create an obstacle or keep someone from seeing the One True God.

Anyway, so that's where I am at the moment. Who knows what next month will look like!

UPDATE: (3/2006)

That was as of 1/25/2005. The "Apology to the World" was written in February, 2005. The business started to flip upside down in March and April resulting in a migration of people leaving the business that were Christians, but couldn't live on faith quite THAT much. We started having prayer meetings in the store, as the Lord directed. Then the Lord led us to start accepting donations of food and toys and clothes and furniture and other things at the furniture store and caring for the poor - which has mushroomed into something amazing. The Church of Liberty website went up in June, 2005. Things got REALLY freaky in October, 2005. Now they're just completely off the charts!

People come to a furniture store to get healing and deliverance and groceries and prayer - or just a hug. More people keep showing up to help. Now we have authors and poets and musicians and artists telling us God gave them something and He told them to give it to ME so we could get it to the world! Miracles happen every day around here. It's just not uncommon at all for a customer to come in and find two or three people on their faces crying. Praise God! I could have never imagined a wilder adventure!

Pray to be dangerous to satan. Pray to get everything out of the way between you and God. Pray that He would bust out of the box you put Him in and reveal Himself in whatever way He thinks best. Stop telling Him what He can and can't do. Let Him talk to you and He'll direct your paths in EVERY way. And I GUARANTEE you that He'll make sure that you stop conforming to the world!

MORE UPDATES: (1/2007)

In July of 2006, God dramatically closed the furniture store and said to walk away. In September my wife moved out and took the kids. The house got foreclosed on. Lots of bills unpaid. God says He'll take care of it all and I'm on HIS time-clock from now on. As of October 2006 God said to hit the road, so I've been traveling all over the country praying and meeting folks and breaking things in the spirit. Sometimes alone, sometimes with a brother traveling along. Sometimes picking up hitch hikers! God is lighting up people all over and I get to watch! He's restoring the Body and bring connectivity and harmony back. Maybe you don't see it yet, but I do! It's coming. The New Song is being played! Praise God and it's just in time.

MORE UPDATES (3/21/2007)

On February 21, 2007, my road trip ended. Total was 17,500 miles to 32 states. Amazing trip, totally dependent on God for every dollar and every direction. Finally got to see my daughters after nearly five months. God said to let my goatee grow until my family is restored. Somehow it all has to do with His Bride and His kids, too. We're walking this one together, trying to get our houses in proper divine order.

Since February 21, God has been having me fan the fires in Liberty with lots of praying and fasting and listening. I spent a lot of time blowing on other people's flames, now it's time to get a blaze going here at home. On April 1, we're going to have the "Liberty Restoration." I have no idea what that means or what it will end up looking like, but God named it, He's organizing it and He'll have His way. I just know that it's time to take "church" outside the walls and BE the Body. If I had to describe what this is that we're going to do, I'd have to call it battlefield triage for a town. I think we're going to set up a M*A*S*H in the city park and treat the wounds of everyone that comes – whether physical, emotional, mental or spiritual. We'll see what that does to the spiritual temperature around here. :-) Stay tuned! I think this is the big one! I thought I was ready after those first 12 weeks and knew what I was doing, but BOY, was I wrong!! Not until NOW did I know how to rest and get out of His way. Just in time!

MORE UPDATES (10/1/2011)

In the summer of 2007 we rented our first townhouse and started inviting folks in need to stay with us. Then we got another and another. At the peak, we had six houses and were the largest homeless shelter in the Northland of Kansas City. We started a food pantry out of the garage and distributed 500,000 pounds of food the first year. People started finding us online and coming for prayer and deliverance from all over the world. I always believed that a big revival was imminent, but I didn't see that revival and restoration is a snowball rolling along and getting bigger and bigger, not an instant event. Most people don't notice until the snowball is really big, but for someone watching closely, it was a long journey to get there. Now we have seven houses, a farm, feeding over 5,000 people every month and ministering to millions on the internet. More people are coming all the time. As of November, 2011, the seven books that I've written will be on Amazon.com as well. It's been a wild ride, and I still feel like it just started.

Quick Thought

How much treasure in heaven are you getting per dollar you're spending on the current ministries you are supporting? What is your return on investment?

When you stand before Jesus and He says,

**"I was hungry and you didn't feed me,
I was naked and you didn't clothe me."**

-- you will NOT be able to say,

**"But Lord, I paid the pastor to do it and
he promised he'd take care of it!"**

It's up to YOU to invest all your spiritual and material resources wisely and be His hands and feet.

You can't outsource your obedience.

If your current ministry investment vehicles are losers, then dump them and find somewhere to invest that will pay a better dividend in heavenly treasure.

You're going to have to look Jesus in the eye and answer for every DIME and every MINUTE!

MESSAGE TO MY BAPTISTS

Brethren, please know that I come from where you come from. My Southern Baptist heritage goes back generations. I'm the son of a pastor and missionary. My dad was a trustee at Midwestern Theological Seminary and Vice President of the Missouri Baptist Convention at one point. I have a religion degree from a Baptist college. I taught Sunday School and sat on committees at one of the largest SBC churches in Missouri. I've got lots of notches on my belt from mission trips, choir tours, summer camps and more.

I didn't leave because someone hurt me. I'm not disgruntled or upset. I just wanted more Jesus than I was getting. Whatever happened to Peter between denying Christ three times and then preaching his first sermon and 3,000 people get dramatically saved - well, I missed that somewhere.

I read about Christians in other places and how they do things. Did you know that the Christians in China are under such persecution that in some places they don't even tell each other when the next meeting is going to be? They just pray and the Holy Spirit tells them all where to meet and when - then ten minutes before the police show up, the Holy Spirit says, "RUN!" and they all run. And they've been doing it that way for fifty years and there has never been any growth close to it in the history of the church. Over 10,000 people a day are coming to Christ in China. It's nothing for them to see amazing healings and miracles and even people raised from the dead. I have friends that travel and minister through Africa and Indonesia and they've SEEN people regrow limbs and interviewed people raised from the dead.

No buildings, no billboards, no TV shows, no direct mail campaigns, no demographic studies, no Purpose Driven stuff, no fancy sound systems - just the Holy Spirit running things. And an expectation that He can speak to them, that He can heal them, that He can provide all that's needed. Walking daily with Jesus is a reality to them, an undeniable relationship - not a figurative possibility or a future hope.

I don't want to give you choices. Jesus didn't give people many choices. Either He was the Son of God or He was a raving, megalomaniacal, lunatic. No middle ground, He painted them into a corner. So if I want to be like Jesus, I probably shouldn't give you many options either. Either I'm right and I'm hearing God OR I'm a dangerous, raving loony. I don't want you to think I'm a nice, but confused, guy. I want you to get fully on board or persecute me. I don't have time for lukewarm anymore - and neither does Jesus.

So here goes ... All the stuff in the Book of Acts is for real and it's for today. You can't pick and choose which of the Gifts of the Spirit are real and for today and which ran out of steam when the Bible was finished being written. Either they're ALL good and available or NONE of them are. So, is there still a Gift of Wisdom? Knowledge? Discernment? You can't just eliminate the uncomfortable ones! I'm telling you from my personal experience - ALL of it is available to you RIGHT NOW. And it sure works a whole lot better than what we've been doing. When someone comes face to face with Almighty God in a great big way, they don't need near as much baby-sitting and enticing to keep coming to church! When they hear the Shepherd's voice for themselves, we don't really have to tell them what to do. If the Holy Spirit is supposed to be our teacher, how is He going to do that if you refuse to hear Him? If there is a war between Good and Evil and Headquarters yells, "DUCK!" but you can't hear it, you're going to be the first casualty - and I don't want to be in a foxhole with you.

I just allowed the possibility that God doesn't change and that what He used to do, He probably would still like to be doing if I would just get my head out of the way. The Word says we're to be FILLED with the Holy Spirit and I didn't feel like my cup was all the way full. I didn't really have peace and joy and victory, because I wasn't really free of sin. Actually the Greek means "to be being filled" - a constant and repeated action - not just a one-time thing. I just prayed that God would fill me so full that nothing else could fit and that He could do whatever with me that He wanted from there. If there is a war between Good and Evil, I don't want a handgun, I want a nuke. Lord, I promise I'll be good, please just give me the big weapons.

Then I saw everything in the book of Acts start to happen right in front of me - right in my little furniture store. All of it - wisdom, words of knowledge, faith, healing, miracles, prophecy, discerning of spirits, tongues, and interpretation of tongues. I've talked to people personally who were given the gift of tongues and it's a specific language of man. I know people from other countries that were given ENGLISH! I've seen people instantly healed of migraines, stomach troubles, hip problems, chronic pain, lupus, fibromyalgia and more. I've seen people oppressed by demons be instantly delivered of fear, anger, confusion, bitterness, addiction, lust, worry, schizophrenia, and more. At one point, we were having a private prayer meeting at the store and while we were praying someone ritually sacrificed a cat in front - right on the main drag in the middle of town on a Tuesday night! No question about it - slit throat, puddle of blood. One of the ladies at the prayer meeting had come out of witchcraft and knew just what it was. She came in and told me and I did a little jig! They didn't understand but I was just so thrilled that we got somebody's attention!! I had never been a part of a church where somebody cursed it and sacrificed an animal out front! If there is a war but nobody is shooting at you - then you're NOT dangerous!

Just work the logic with me here. There is a war and the enemy has witches and spells and astral projection and zombies and voodoo and mediums and psychics and channeling and talking to demons. That stuff IS for real and has impact on the "natural" world - to varying degrees. Even Christians that don't believe God speaks to people, won't play with a Ouija board – because SOMETHING will answer you!

So where's MY stuff? This is a war in which they have all these weapons and all our stuff ended when the Bible was completed? Whose idea was that?! Who is most glorified by the theology that our God doesn't speak anymore and all the cool stuff He promised us and we see in play in Acts (and following) is no good anymore? Surely it must have been satan's idea because it sure makes Jesus look kind of neutered.

Why does only one side get cool weapons? Was my denomination leaving out important stuff that I needed for warfare? Because in the first century they had amazing weapons and defenses available to them. They had the Holy Spirit telling them stuff they wouldn't have known (Acts 5:1-11), they had people hearing from God (Acts 13:2), they had people writing stuff as God dictated and prophesying about the future (Revelation), they were caught up in the Spirit to heaven (2 Corin. 12:2-4), they had dreams and visions (Acts 10:9-23), they saw angels (Acts 12), they saw Jesus Himself (Acts 9:1-22), they cast out demons (Acts 16:16-18), they were bitten by deadly snakes and didn't die (Acts 28:1-10), they spoke in other languages of men and of angels (Acts 2, I Corin. 12 & more), they healed people (Acts 5:15), they prayed and miracles happened (Acts 5:12, Acts 12) – even teleportation (Acts 8:39) and they raised the dead (Acts 9:32-42)! They even had people who were against them drop dead (Acts 5:1-11) or go blind (Acts 13:6-12) – on command! (And that's just ONE reference for each! There are lots more!)

And it can't just be about the Apostles, because there were people doing some of this stuff in the Old Testament, too. So the Holy Spirit didn't first appear on the scene at Pentecost and then disappear when the Bible was completed. That just makes no sense. Not to mention that it flies in the face of millions of Christians around the world that are walking in the power of Christ, not just the salvation of Christ.

The Baptists taught me the Word really well, taught me to love Jesus, and taught me discernment and skepticism. That stuff is important because there are many false prophets and false revivals out there – and more coming (including one really big, one world religion). I'm not a sucker for whatever stupid manifestation-seeking fad comes along. I want 100% pure Jesus. It just that I've learned that we left some important stuff out. I'm just pretty sure that I grieved the Holy Spirit for a lot of years by telling God what He did and didn't do anymore. It says if we bind it on earth it will be bound in heaven. If you don't believe God can talk to you, He probably won't. If you don't think God can heal people, then put your trust in doctors and pray God will help them remember what they learned in school. It just seems kind of sad and useless to have a prayer meeting where we all bow our heads while somebody reads off the names of all the sick people, but none of us actually believe God will do anything miraculous.

My God is bigger. My God doesn't change. Please, Brothers, I love you all, but stop putting Him in a box. Let Him be God. Expect Him to be true to ALL His promises. Seek more. There's more to be had. I promise.

WHERE ARE THE MARTYRS?

What if Walmart said, "Trust us, just give us a percentage of your gross income and we'll spend it wisely. You'll get a good product. We promise." Would you believe them? Don't you think there are market forces at work in the church? That they would look for efficiencies and start cutting corners?

That is, if I were the pastor of a church of 1,000 people and I preached six weeks in a row about the dangers of riches and the judgement on the wealthy and the need to pick up our cross daily and the complete inadequacy of a little prayer when you were eight if you've never since lived your life with holiness - do you think I would still have 1,000 people at the end of the six weeks? Do you think I would have a job?

See, WE'RE the consumers! As long as we spend the money there will always be someone willing to tickle our ears. Most of the time, they don't even know they're doing it.

No way, boys. Not anymore. Not with MY money. We are seeing NEGATIVE population growth in the church. We are NOT feeding the hungry. We are not caring for the orphans. We are not reaching the lost. We're not even keeping up with population growth. We are bringing in $250 BILLION a year and spending 95% of it on comforts and programs for the "saved". AND we're in debt up to our eyeballs!!

THIS IS NO KIND OF WAY TO FIGHT A WAR!

So I say, accept personal responsibility (as I have) for having fed this beast. If your church is soft and fluffy - DON'T throw more money at it hoping it will start saying hard things - the money is what made them want to BE soft and fluffy! If your church is saying the hard things and meeting needs and doing God's work the way God wants it done - then give them ALL your money! He'll give you more.

Where are the martyrs?! Where are the people willing to do anything for the cause of Christ?! We need them to get to work. Something big is coming. God's given us the vision and laid out the plan. All the pieces are coming together.

All the people in the wilderness need to hook up, get fed some real meat and then we need to send them BACK into the churches with big armloads of meat to show love and feed the hungry. If we can get little tornadoes of revival started and they get some critical mass, eventually people are going to go up to the pastor and ask him to preach something hard for a change - and THEN he will be unshackled and free to say what he's aching to say, but been taught (by us) not to!

If God tells you to stay in the "church" then stay – and speak the Truth in love. But don't assume you're going to get fed meat there, you might not. But stay because you love them – and just ask lots questions.

Lean over to someone next to you in the service and gently and very sweetly say something like:

- Hey, did we pray about that new building? Whose idea was it?

- Hmmm. I wonder if there's another way to reach people?

- I wonder why there aren't more minorities here?

- I wonder what would happen if a smelly, homeless guy wanted to come to church here?

- I wonder what Jesus would have thought of that sermon?

- Ever think there must be more to it than this?

- When was the last time you saw anybody really repenting around here?

We need covert, special forces commandos to fulfill Romans 12 until we can get the whole army ready to fight.

That's the simple three step plan for warfare on God's terms.

If in thanks for His mercy, you're willing to offer your Bodies (personal, family, congregation, town - any or all of them) as living sacrifices, holy and pleasing to God (that means washed clean and acceptable) - do THIS:

1. STOP CONFORMING TO THE PATTERN OF THE WORLD!!!!

For Pete's sake! We were never supposed to get comfy here! We were never supposed to go into the land of milk and honey and leave God in the desert! (Ex. 33!) We're to be aliens in a strange land. We're to be fools for Jesus. We're to be hated and despised! Whose idea could it have been to have 37,000+ denominations and feuding and fighting and waste and fraud and hypocrisy and compromise and building consultants and demographic experts??!!! Can you say, "Sataaaan?"

2. Be transformed by the RENEWING of your minds.

Grow up into Him who is the Head. Get all the junk OUT and focus on JESUS!! Every man-made thing is DROSS! It's chaff. It's rubbish. IT WILL SURELY BURN OFF IN THE FIRE! The only pure, clean truth is the WORD. Learn Jesus, do what Jesus wants, ignore what Jesus would have ignored, love who Jesus loved. Stop reading the 1,000 Man-made commentaries on the book of Hebrews and read HEBREWS and beg the Spirit to show you what you need! Get as much Holy Spirit in you as you can, as fast as you can. Pray for wisdom! That's at the top of all the lists of gifts, seems to be the least likely to get abused and what seems to be lacking most right now. You don't need Forty Days of Purpose to figure out what you want to do for God - you're the SACRIFICE! Just get up on the altar and shut up! If you'll just lay there and stop squirming, when He is good and ready, He'll cut your head off and put His head on. Then your mind will be RE-newed. Back the way it was supposed to be. Rebooted to His default settings and conformed to Christ. Oh, and get sanctified so you'll be an acceptable sacrifice - and don't bring your baggage up on the altar.

3. THEN you will know what is the perfect will of God - AND THEN DO IT!

It's not theoretical - it's ACTION. Find out what God wants and DO IT. No more need for demographic studies and committee meetings and long-range plans. You'll KNOW the perfect will of God because you have His head! And I GUARANTEE it will look different than what we've BEEN doing.

There's more, but that's the big thing. You can ONLY find repentance and revival and restoration by those three - in that order.

Then, once you're hearing God really well, go back into the churches and heap burning coals of conviction on their heads by feeding them the meat they are dying for and the water they are thirsting for. Be Christ to them. God is preparing MANY hearts. People I thought unredeemable are asking questions again. The harvest is white.

Ask lots of questions, show love, bring them to small groups inside or outside the church where they can be challenged and grow. Don't expect to feed people individually and disciple them in groups of a thousand.

That's what we're hoping to see - a massive, self-replicating, mobile, cellular, no-nonsense structure that can operate inside or outside the church walls (and survive any persecution) to reinforce and restore and urge others toward Christ.

Read Judges 6. God calls Gideon to save Israel from the Midianites, but before he can go do that, he has to take care of the idolatry in his own backyard!! So he calls TEN friends together and they go in covertly at night (very shrewd - frontal assault won't work) and switch Baal's altar to an altar for God and then use the Asherah pole as the fuel for the sacrifice to God. They used the assets of the idolatry as the fuel to accomplish something for the Kingdom!! I love that part!

In the morning the men are mad and want to kill Gideon, but his Dad talks them down. Now ... I think they gave up too easily if they really loved Baal. They're trying to save face and they hate change, but I suspect at least some of those Jews thought, "You know, this really is better anyway. We should have done this a long time ago. Wish I'd have had the chutzpah to do that!" Just a couple chapters later, they want Gideon to be ruler over them! Give me 11 good people willing to die for Christ, hearing God's voice clearly, trained to show love, speaking only pure Truth, shrewd as serpents, harmless as doves, and determined to make a difference - and see what kind of impact they could have on a congregation or a town!

THEN Gideon can blow the trumpet and mass 32,000 and go fight the larger enemies rallied against God. And he needed all 32,000. The ones that went home weren't just chicken, they had responsibilities and families and businesses and infrastructure that the tribe needed to maintain. God knows that. He wasn't mad at them. But notice Judges 7:8. Gideon sends 31,700 of them home, but they leave ALL their provisions! That's the way God's economy should be working. The folks on the front lines doing battle up close with the enemy need to have SO much provision and supplies that they can meet any need - feed any that are hungry, give to any that are thirsty.

Those 1% on the front lines hearing God clearly are people that have proven they can be trusted to use assets for the Kingdom - those willing to die for Christ aren't going to buy a BENTLEY!! I'm sorry, they're just not.

I know folks working with prostitutes and drug addicts and runaways and gangs - and hardly anybody is supporting them. There is a giant underground church of ex-skinheads and witches and satanists and gang-bangers that will not even TALK to a Christian in a cardigan or set foot in a church for how toxic it is to them! They're pushing back the darkness in the worst conditions and getting NO help at all. Do we not care about the down and out? The unreached? Didn't Jesus?

Think of it this way, if God let's you and your kids stay home in the suburbs and keep your job and somebody else will go hold the heads of the junkies and clean up the prostitutes and tell them about Jesus - what's it worth to you?

Which do you think results in more treasure in heaven?

New chandelier in the sanctuary <--------> or getting 14 year old girls off the streets and into heaven?

Tithing because a guy in a suit says you HAVE to <---------> or Reaching those who have NEVER ONCE in their whole lives heard the name of Jesus spoken in their presence?

Your new $3000 big screen TV <---------> or Feeding 60 orphans in Ghana for a YEAR?

Consider I Corinthians 14:8

"Again, if the trumpet make an uncertain sound, who will prepare for the battle?"

We've got nothing BUT uncertain sounds -- if there are any at all!

I've got no patience anymore for anything that isn't 100% about Jesus.

No more messing around. This is WAR!

Where are the people willing to die so that Christ in them can live?

Where are the REAL Christians?!

WHERE ARE THE MARTYRS?!

HELP WANTED – CITY RESTORATION POSITIONS AVAILABLE

WANTED: Christians that want restoration of the Body of Christ more than anything else.

PRIMARY JOB: To help bring in the last great harvest.

TITLE: KOGS (Kingdom of God Servants) - sometimes also referred to as "cogs"

NUMBER OF POSITIONS AVAILABLE: Unlimited - but currently we are pitifully understaffed for the size of the harvest we're predicting.

QUALIFICATIONS: They need to have no other gods before Me. They need to have My heart (hungry, naked, poor, in prison, etc.). They are going to need to be willing to receive with open arms and hearts the Outside Consultants and Management Experts that I send to them for training and correction purposes. They must be willing to lay down any flawed traditions or businesses practices that they have been using up to this point, so that I can retrain them. They must want to hear My voice so that I can direct their paths. They must stop putting Me in a box and asking Me to endorse THEIR ideas. They must want to be One Body with all the other KOGS and stop fighting with each other.

We are an equal opportunity employer, but priority hiring goes to those in the following categories: widows, orphans, handicapped, limping, poor, naked, down-trodden, bankrupt, criminals, prostitutes, tax-collectors, common laborers (especially carpenters and fishermen) and other broken, flawed vessels who have been humbled already. Rich people and seminary graduates may have to undergo additional breaking in order to qualify. Anyone willing to truly lay down their life (and stuff) for a friend goes to the front of the line.

REMUNERATIONS: Those accepting this position will get to see the Spirit of God descend in power on their assembly and their town like never before. They will get to see Me walk in their midst. They will learn peace and joy and victory on a scale they didn't know possible and they will have true community for the first time. They will also be ridiculed and persecuted - but they won't care. I will individually and collectively lift them up onto My lap and rub their head and wipe away every tear. I will pay all their bills and take care of their every need. I will be their Daddy.

APPLICATION PROCESS: If you have previously been revived for any period of time, before applying again you need to first say you're sorry for losing what was given to you previously. We can't give you a fresh fire until you repent for letting the last one go out. (Weeping and mourning is helpful in convincing us of your sincerity.) If you are new to this and have never made application before, just fill out the form below and submit by fervent prayer.

DEADLINE: This vacancy will remain open until we find qualified candidates or until the harvest is over. But time is getting short, so you might want to hurry before you miss it.

NOTE: Those who are comfortable with the current state of things and/or unrepentant for their part in the pain and suffering around them need not apply. Please refer to Ezekiel 9 for clarification. Church leaders please refer to Ezekiel 34.

For available positions in your area find someone that is feeding the hungry, clothing the naked, visiting prisoners, etc. They have a direct line to Headquarters.

CITY RESTORATION APPLICATION FORM:

Name: _____

Jesus Preference: (check all that apply)

___ Emergency-Only Jesus   ___ Church Growth Jesus
___ Prosperity Jesus   ___ Denominational Jesus

___ Fire-Insurance-Get-Out-Of-Hell-Free Jesus

___ Nonjudgemental-Everybody-Goes-To-Heaven Jesus
___ Didn't-Come-In-The-Flesh Jesus

___ Loves-Me-But-Can't/Won't-Talk-To-Me Jesus

___ Not-Quite-As-Good-As-The-Virgin-Mary Jesus

___ Nice-Philosopher/Prophet-But-Not-Divine Jesus

___ Master, King, Commander, Lord Jesus

___ Other:_____

SCREENING QUESTIONS:

Money: (Check One)

___ I owe God 10% of my money.

___ I owe God 10% of my money and an occasional love gift or offering.

___ I owe God everything I have and none of it is really mine.

Time: (Check One)

___ People have been saying for years that He is coming, why hurry?

___ People have been saying for years that He is coming, I should move faster.

___ He is coming soon! I can't waste a second!

Sacrifice: (Check One)

___ I am willing to give up Sunday mornings and Wednesday nights.

___ I am willing to be substantially inconvenienced on a regular basis.

___ I am willing to die for Jesus.

Love: (Check One)

___ I love the people in my family (mostly).

___ I love the people that are like me and agree with me.

___ I love my enemies (and my family and the people that agree with me).

Humility: (Check One)

___ Mine is the Kingdom

___ Mine is the Power

___ Mine is the Glory

___ Thine is the Kingdom and the Power and the Glory forever.

Prayer: (Check One)

___ I close my eyes when other people are praying and try to pay attention.

___ I often pray in front of people and I pray at home by myself.

___ I pray without ceasing, often alone crying out to God and with tears and supplications.

Availability Date: (Check One)

___ When I'm retired and mostly out of steam anyway.

___ When I'm perfect and feel worthy.

___ Whenever He says He wants me. Right NOW would be nice.

Please consider me for this position. I'm willing to go anywhere, do anything, endure anything, give anything, unlearn anything, pray without ceasing, be instant in season and out of season, know the Word of God and obey His commands and learn to hear His voice. I know I can't get there on my own and I'm sorry I ever tried. I will let Him direct ALL my paths from now on and I won't lean on my own understanding anymore. I will happily receive everything that I'm going to need to be fully equipped for His purposes. I'm ready to start anytime.

Signed: _____

OFFICE USE ONLY: Qualified? ____ Start Date? ____

End Date? ____ Rich Welcome Scheduled? ____

HELP WANTED – CITY RESTORATION LEADERSHIP POSITIONS AVAILABLE

WANTED: Christian leaders that want the restoration of the Body of Christ more than anything else and are willing to do whatever it takes regardless of the cost.

PRIMARY JOB: To help bring in the last great harvest and to serve God's people selflessly.

TITLE: L.O.T. (Least of These) - sometimes also referred to as "humble servants."

NUMBER OF POSITIONS AVAILABLE: Unlimited - but currently are pitifully understaffed for the size of the harvest we're predicting.

QUALIFICATIONS: They need to have no other gods before Me. They need to have My heart (for the hungry, naked, poor, in prison, etc.). They are going to need to be willing to receive with open arms and hearts the Outside Consultants and Management Experts that I send to them for training and correction purposes – but test everything. They must be willing to lay down any flawed traditions or business practices that they have been using up to this point, so that I can retrain them. They must want to hear My voice so that I can direct their paths. They must stop putting Me in a box and asking Me to endorse THEIR ideas. They must want to be One Body and stop fighting with each other.

We are an equal opportunity employer, but priority hiring goes to those in the following categories: widows, orphans, handicapped, limping, poor, naked, down-trodden, bankrupt, criminals, prostitutes, tax-collectors, common laborers (especially carpenters and fishermen) and other broken, flawed vessels who have been humbled already. Rich people and seminary graduates may have to undergo additional breaking in order to qualify. Anyone willing to truly lay down their life (and stuff) for a friend goes to the front of the line. If they are not willing to cry repentantly in front of others and be transparent, they won't be able to lead the sheep to Me.

REMUNERATIONS: Those accepting this position will get to see the Spirit of God descend in power on their assembly and their town like never before. They will get to see Me walk in their midst. They will learn peace and joy and victory and intimacy with Me on a scale they didn't know possible and they will have true community for the first time. I will pay all their bills and take care of their every need. I will hold their hand.

COSTS: It's very important that they count the cost ahead of time. If they accept this position they will be ridiculed and persecuted. It will probably result in the loss of some or all of the following: prestige, health, leisure time, money and assets of all kinds, home – even spouse and children are at risk. Those who accept this position will be beat on and reshaped and refined on a scale they can't even imagine, but I promise to never let it go beyond what they can handle. Their success will be directly proportional to their willingness to let My refining fire burn off everything in them that stands in the way of My plans. It WILL absolutely, positively hurt a LOT – but I will personally wipe away their every tear. In the end, they will look like Me – and I will treat them as a Father treats his Son..

APPLICATION PROCESS: Submit this application with fear and trembling and ask Me to do whatever it takes to make you ready right NOW no matter how much it hurts. Then bite down on something.

DEADLINE: This vacancy will remain open until we find qualified candidates or until the harvest is over. But if you're supposed to be leading and you refuse, the blood of all the people that didn't get reached because you wouldn't stand up in the day of battle (or move fast enough) is on YOU. So you might want to hurry. **NOTE: If you need extra motivation, please read Ezekiel 34 several times out loud.**

For available positions in your area find someone that has lost everything and has been thoroughly beaten into submission. They have a direct line to Headquarters.

CITY RESTORATION LEADERSHIP APPLICATION FORM:

Name: _____

Jesus Preference: (check all that apply)

___ Emergency-Only Jesus   ___ Prosperity Jesus

___ Denominational Jesus   ___ Church Growth Jesus

___ Fire-Insurance-Get-Out-Of-Hell-Free Jesus

___ Nonjudgemental-Everybody-Goes-To-Heaven Jesus

___ Didn't-Come-In-The-Flesh Jesus

___ Loves-Me-But-Can't/Won't-Talk-To-Me Jesus

___ Master, King, Commander, Lord Jesus

___ Other:_____

SCREENING QUESTIONS:

Money: (Check One)

___ I am willing to go, so long as I know a regular paycheck is coming and I have some security.

___ I am willing to go and live on faith, so long as I can tell people about my needs.

___ I am willing to go and live on faith and depend on God alone and never mention my needs to anyone.

Service: (Check One)

___ I am willing to serve those who will really appreciate what I do and won't ask me to get too dirty.

___ I am willing to serve even if no one notices, so long as I can feel like we're making some progress.

___ I am willing to serve those who will beat me and spit on me, and I won't stop even if it never pays off.

Prayer: (Check One)

___ I often stand in front and make long flowery prayers to impress people.

___ I frequently intercede for others and spend lots of hours alone in prayer.

___ I pray without ceasing and offer to stand in the gap and take on me anything necessary to free another.

Sacrifice: (Check One)

___ I am willing to strain my tea and religiously give 10% of all my spices and other garden produce.

___ I am willing to give all that I have, but I'd like to make payments and spread it out over time.

___ I am willing to die to self – all at once right now or in big chunks every day – regardless of the pain.

Humility: (Check One)

___ I prefer the seats of honor at the front and try to make sure everyone knows where I belong.

___ Mine is the Kingdom

___ Mine is the Power

___ Mine is the Glory

___ Thine is the Kingdom and the Power and the Glory forever. I'll take the crumbs from under the table.

Urgency: (Check One)

___ I will go when I'm sure that I'm fully prepared and know all that I need to know to be effective.

___ I will go right now, but I refuse to go over 20 miles per hour so as not to get hurt too bad in an accident.

___ I already left and I'm going 200 miles per hour and I don't care what happens, I'm not slowing down.

Determination: (Check One)

___ I will persevere until someone raises an eyebrow or threatens to leave my church.

___ I will persevere until it starts costing me things I really love.

___ I will persevere until someone kills me and I get to go Home.

Please consider me for this position. I'm willing to go anywhere, do anything, endure anything, give anything, unlearn anything, pray without ceasing, be instant in season and out of season, know the Word of God and obey His commands and learn to hear His voice. I know I can't get there on my own and I'm sorry I ever tried. I will let Him direct ALL my paths from now on and I won't lean on my own understanding anymore. I will happily receive everything that I'm going to need to be fully equipped for His purposes. I promise to never make it about me. I'm ready to start anytime.

Signed: _____

OFFICE USE ONLY:

Qualified? ____ Start Date? ____ End Date? ____

Rich Welcome Scheduled? ____ Robe Size? ____

*"OK, so the whole thing is a mess.
What do we DO about it?"*

www.TheChurchOfLiberty.com

**The City Church is the only thing that will
work. It's the only thing in the Bible.
And it's coming.**

Other books that might help you:

"Rain Right NOW, Lord!" - All about Spiritual
Gifts and how to keep your cup so full of
Jesus that nothing else can fit!

www.FellowshipOfTheMartyrs.com/rain_down_now.htm

"The Red Dragon" – Why the church
CANNOT seem to change.

www.FellowshipOfTheMartyrs.com/red_dragon.htm

"Who Neutered the Holy Spirit?" - What
happened to God?

www.FellowshipOfTheMartyrs.com/neutered.htm

And much more on the website.

For other similar books and materials and for the most radical anointed music, art, T-shirts, buttons, stickers, books and more, shop our online store.

All proceeds devoted to pushing back the darkness in the most efficient possible way.

www.FellowshipOfTheMartyrs.com
www.TheChurchOfLiberty.com

Post to: Fellowship Of The Martyrs
118 N. Conistor, #B251
Liberty, MO 64068

Email to: fotm@fellowshipofthemartyrs.com
if we can help in any way.

Thank you, Father, for this opportunity to reach out and touch the life of another. Please let them receive everything in this book that you have for them. Please keep the enemy from distracting them and closing up their hearts and minds. Lord, bring Your spirit of repentance on us and on our land. In the Name of Jesus, Amen.

Need More Jesus? Pray THIS!

"Jesus, I'm really sorry for the mess I've made of my life, my family, my town, my country and my planet. I don't deserve it, but would You please straighten it all out before it's too late? I promise I'll let

You drive from now on and I'll sit in the back seat and shut up. Please just don't leave me like this. I stink at this. I just want YOU, Jesus! Please get anything that stands between me and You out of the way and tell me what to do. Give me wisdom and teach me to fear You and to obey you only. Fill me so full of Your Spirit that nothing else can fit. I'll take whatever you want to give me. I love you. In the mighty Name of my Lord Jesus Christ. Amen."

Want to be REALLY dangerous? Pray THIS!

(WARNING!! This WILL hurt. He WILL answer it. Guaranteed!)

"Lord, whatever it takes, whatever the cost, crush me, kill me, crucify me, break me, humble me, rip everything away from me, do whatever you want to me - just make me dangerous to the enemy in the biggest possible way. I understand that means I need to have more of YOU than I have now. Do whatever it takes. Give me a bigger cup of Jesus and keep it all the way full. I trust you and I love you, King Jesus. I'll hang in there. And please do it right NOW! In the Name of my Lord Jesus Christ. Amen."

ABOUT THE AUTHOR

Doug Perry has been going 200 miles an hour with his hair on fire since November 23, 2004 when God showed him an open vision of how much God loves His children, how angry God is for how we're killing His children, and how much we have to hurry. It's safe to say that praying to see through the eyes of Jesus and be dangerous to satan wrecked his life. He had a nice home, a wife, two kids, two dogs, a foreign car with a sunroof, and a multimillion dollar, award-winning business that was named the #4 fastest growing company in Kansas City in 2006. Shoot, he was even teaching Sunday School.

Then he realized what he was, what we've built, and how it looks in the light of holiness. He realized he was a friend of the world – and an enemy of God. (James 4:4) So he sold all he had and gave it to the poor – or it was stripped from him one way or another.

And it was all worth it.

Now he's the author of seven books, nearly a thousand videos, music, poetry, and founder of a homeless shelter and a food pantry that feeds 5,000+ people every month. He has cried on the sidewalk in public for days. He's been arrested on false charges. He's spent weeks at a time in prayer, fasting and weeping for the sad state of things.

And he's been spit on, lied about, abandoned, forsaken by friends, banned by pastors, ejected from sanctuaries – and looks more like Jesus all the time. He's even had people try to physically kill him! Just for speaking the hard truth nobody wants to hear. But Jesus said it would be like that. Praise God! Bring it on.
If nobody is shooting at you, then you're <u>not</u> dangerous.

OTHER TITLES FROM
FELLOWSHIP OF THE MARTYRS

Rain Right <u>NOW</u>, Lord! - from Doug Perry
What is it going to take for God to pour His Spirit out on all flesh? Or is He waiting for us? Are spiritual gifts real and for today – and how do you get more of them?

The Apology to the World – from Doug Perry
The "Apology to the World" letter has influenced thousands and been all over the world. This book spawned from responses to that letter and collected writings about the need for change.

Left-Handed Warriors – from Linda Carriger
A suspenseful tale of the supernatural vs. the natural. What was it like for kids growing up in the book of Acts? Linda paints a picture of what it's like to be radically sold out to Christ – and still a kid.

Missionaries are Human, Too – from Nancy Perry
A sweet, candid look at what it's like to be a missionary family learning to trust God in a foreign country. Written in 1976.

Dialogues With God – from Doug Perry
Some discussions between Doug and the Almighty, along with a trouble-shooting guide to help you get unclogged, get your cup full and hear God better.

DEMONS?! You're kidding, right? - from Doug Perry
A very detailed guide to spiritual warfare – how the bad guys act, what they look like, where they hide and much more. For experts only. Not for sissies. Seriously. We're not kidding.

Do It Yourself City Church Restoration – from **Doug Perry**

What was 'church' supposed to be like all along? Are we doing it right? What's it going to take to fix it? If Jesus Christ wrote a letter to the Body of Christ in your city, could you bear to read it? What would happen if you were One Body in your town?

Who Neutered the Holy Spirit?! - from **Doug Perry**

Why do people say that the Holy Spirit stopped doing all the cool stuff that used to happen? This details the scriptural evidence of the work of the Spirit in the Old Testament, in the New Testament, after Pentecost, and in the church today. Along with help to get you unclogged so you can walk in the fullness of what God has for you.

The Red Dragon: the horrifying truth about why the 'church' cannot seem to change – from **Doug Perry**

How bad are things? How did they get this bad? In fact, they're SO bad, they have to be considered supernaturally bad! In fact, it's a curse from God. A delusion sent on those that went their own way. Weep. No really, weep! That's your only hope.

Expelling Xavier – from **Dorothy Haile**

A love story between a girl possessed by something dark and a boy just learning who he is in Christ – and their Savior. A very different kind of Christian novel, gritty, rough and fiercely transparent about the realities of life under the control of the darkness.

The Big Picture Book – from **Doug Perry**

Coming soon. Answers to some of the DEEP questions.

And LOTS more titles coming soon!!
And in SPANISH!